THE ENDANGERED SALES PERSON'S PATH TO LONGEVITY

The Endangered Sales Person's Path to Longevity

John (Doc) Fabiano

THE ENDANGERED SALES PERSON'S PATH TO LONGEVITY

iUniverse books may be ordered through booksellers or by contacting:

iUniverse
1663 Liberty Drive
Bloomington, IN 47403
www.iuniverse.com
1-800-Authors (1-800-288-4677)

ISBN: 978-1-5320-3338-4 (sc)
ISBN: 978-1-5320-3339-1 (e)

Library of Congress Control Number: 2017914603

Print information available on the last page.

iUniverse rev. date: 09/26/2017

DEDICATIONS AND ACKNOWLEDGEMENTS

DEDICATION
FOR
PAT COLLINS AND BOB HAWTHORNE
Great friends and great salesmen and two very different people

AND FOR
Beth, my wife, my best friend, who reminds me daily of the goodness of life with her love, kindness, and empathy towards all.

ACKNOWLEDGEMENT
It has been a long sail from the beginning to reaching a safe harbor, and there have been many who have contributed to the kind of sailor I have become. All have graced me with kindness and the benefit of their experiences and beliefs and I have always been and remain grateful.

Thank you all.

CONTENTS

TAO:

A philosophical system advocating a life of complete simplicity and naturalness and of non-interference with the course of natural events, in order to attain a happy and harmonic existence.

OCCAM'S RAZOR:

In any given situation or problem, it is likely the simplest solution is the best.

It is called a "path", not a "guide". You have to follow a guide, but you get to choose your own path.

###

PREFACE

Now you ask, who am I to write such a book?

Good question.

For over twenty years I was in capital sales (six figure plus deals) for what eventually became a global communications company. In the early years I was a regional manager responsible for shepherding a group of diverse, private distributors into selling my company's products, providing a higher level of customer satisfaction, educating the employees on many subjects, planning for the future, keeping them up to date on industry trends, and in general, managing my charges to assigned targets and margins.

I eventually ascended to the national sales manager position which included every state and Puerto Rico. I still had the same responsibilities as well as guiding (more than managing) my team of outstanding sales representatives in pursuit of their targets and responsibilities.

During all that time, I developed and conducted hundreds of product, sales, and customer service training classes. If I wanted my company's products sold, I needed to be sure those sales people knew the generics of sales first, before learning the specifics of selling the product. Generic sales training came first, followed by training seminars on specific selling techniques, such as financial selling, consultant selling, and collaborative selling.

Being "hands on" I always offered to participate in the sales of my products and, consequently, I experienced sales methods, techniques, strategies, and processes of sales organizations in every state. As a result of my participation and "value-add" approach, at any given time during my tenure, many of my distributors' personnel looked to me for leadership, motivation, information, and sales management. And these people did not work for my company or me.

What I observed and learned from all of this was that the top performers, no matter what state they were in or company they worked for, always based their sales methods on the basics and fundamentals of the generic sales process. Those that did not take the time to learn and perfect the basics as well as record their activities and results, did a poor job of adjusting to the sales "climate" in their area and time.

The top performers worked with a simple base line that I have reduced here to a simple mantra: question, listen, keep it simple, and make it yours.

There is no more concise way to put it.

Here is the true reality:

Sales is not a battle, a war, or an athletic competition, all lay metaphors withstanding. Such assume that the customer is the enemy, the opposition, and is to be defeated implying that the sales person is the winner and the customer is the loser. That doesn't make sense when the object of the exercise is to provide the best and most reasonable solution to satisfy the customer's needs. Sales is a simple process with altruistic overtones and shading and needs not be complicated when reasonable and ethical people collaborate to enact responsible and mutually effective business agreements.

The best sales people I knew across the country operated from this definition.

This book begins with who I have written it for and where the value is. It is followed by an examination of how and why the sales industry has changed, due largely to two factors: a failure to keep current with the changing landscape of the business world and how the explosion of technology continues to make the sales person unnecessary or even obsolete.

There is a simple list of suggested ways to succeed in a rapidly changing business world which is followed by an examination of "The Tao of Sales", which translates to the simplest basics and fundamentals. Combining the two, in your own way, is what will make the difference for you. To perform well in any rapidly changing environment, you must be able to adjust, adapt, and overcome.

Consider all this. Use your brain. Think. Read between the lines as well as the words themselves. Connect your experiences, positive and negative, to what you read. Don't try to do me, verbatim, but make it yours. If it resonates, use it; if it doesn't, find something that will.

You can do this; good sales people, serious sales people, have an organic understanding of what can and needs to be done.

Some time ago, I was delivering one of my seminars to a sales team in the mid-west. It was winter and the snow was falling. I live in Florida and enjoy a tan year round. One of the sales people in the audience said: "Look at your tan; you obviously don't work very hard."

I responded: "You are correct, I don't work very hard. I work smart."

CHAPTER 0

What is the Value to Me?

The sales person may well be an endangered species.

Let us begin with a reader courtesy that is getting right to the point, the heart of the matter, down to brass tacks, and the rag off of the bush: the value of this book.

And that is to assist sales management and sales people, of all sizes, shapes, and levels of experience, in overcoming obstacles and challenges created by the explosion of technology and the rapidly changing landscape of how the world does business.

It is also intended to help sales people improve, because, besides changes connected to the effects of technology, from conclusions determined by studies, reports, and recorded observations, it is clear that not all of the former sales processes, methods, and strategies work as well as they used to. Statistical studies back this up and point directly to areas of concern regarding sales people and buyers, alike. While most of us are not turned on by numbers, it is hard to avoid the fact that two plus two equals four.

It is for sales people and sales managers who are infrequently or barely making targets; who are not driving the car they want, living where and how they would like, and struggling with financial and personal satisfaction and all the while wondering "why?".

Taken in total, this information is a lot to swallow but the sheer volume and consistency of this data cannot be ignored.

Of all employed sales people in this country (approx. 12.3% of the total employed population) studies have indicated that some 55% should not be in sales at all, and of the remaining, 64% are in the wrong sales job. Considering this country spends some one trillion dollars on sales forces annually, one might make the case that half of that is wasted. It follows then, that helping prospective and existing sales people come to the conclusion that either they should not be in sales or are in the wrong sales job, has to have value to the company bottom up in terms of time, potential lost business, and money ill-spent.

Early in the book is a discussion of how to determine if one should be in sales at all which can also be a simple method for sales management to employ to cull the misplaced sales people. There is a suggested, simple, format to follow to assist the employee in determining if the sales job in question is viable, demonstrating whether or not the total compensation at plan is at least enough to meet the sales person's monthly financial needs. This is something I have rarely seen new sales people complete.

As there is a simple formula for the sales person to determine the validity of the job, there is also herein a larger program suitable for all levels of sales management to determine if the extant market is worth pursuing, how many sales people may be required, and what quotas may be validated, calculated from average closing ratios, sales cycle times, average contract value, and similar pieces that may be decimalized simply.

Of the studies researched, 50% of sales managers report they are too busy to train or develop their sales force; 50% of sales people have no planned approach, and 50% of sales people have no playbook. The aforementioned programs may assist sales management in validating plans and the entire book explains that deliberately vetting plans and planning each step of the sales cycle is most prudent.

The average American company spends $12000-$15000 to hire a sales person but only an average of $2000 to train them. It is an indictment that from the start, many sales people begin at a disadvantage.

Nonetheless, a quick review of today's technology demonstrates there are ample capabilities for eliminating valuable time wasted with effective processes that require considerably less time and effort. This technology has also allowed the creation of software that greatly assists prospecting and customer relationship management.

Changes in the business climate have not been lost on a battalion of sales trainers, motivators, and process seminar companies. A quick look at just the first two Google pages of these should have one scratching his or her head. These companies report that they have presented new, sure fire techniques as well as successfully trained and motivated literally thousands and thousands of sales people across the country and each company announces ownership of the number one position.

Thousands and thousands? If that were true, why is it that more than two thirds of the sales people today do not make quota? And again, if that were true, why is it that the major concern sales management has about investing in these events is that, shortly thereafter, many, if not all, of their sales people have either forgotten or do not apply what they experienced at company expense?

The best way to overcome these problems is to re-examine the basics, the fundamentals of the generic sales process as to establish a firm baseline of knowledge upon which the salesperson can re-establish successful methods for today's markets as well as absorb and apply (if found to be resonant) what was presented at the seminars and training events he or she may attend.

The book is based on the philosophy of Tao and Occam's Razor Theory, both of which are grounded in simplicity. It presents and dissects what makes a top performer and examines the steps of the generic sales process, that, regardless of all the psychological and futuristic rhetoric, are difficult to separate from the reality of the process.

A common issue with sales people and sales managers is that they frequently do not see the forest for the trees. Do they know their closing ratio? Do they know how long it takes to close a deal from start to finish? Do they know what the best prospecting methods are for them, as individuals, and do they understand what they do that consistently works and that which does not? Are they being themselves or are they trying to imitate someone else they have seen, perhaps at one of those seminars, who garnered their attention?

The book talks specifically and frequently about taking ownership of whatever needs be done, in an individualistic manner. It further provides a technique and exercise to help the sales person connect with who he or she is and how to make the subject distinctively personal. After all, people buy from people and no one will listen to someone who does not appear to be genuine. The book endeavors to help the sales person evaluate and benefit from the organic capacities he or she may possess. Either it exists or it doesn't

To assist the sales person in self-measurement and self-management is a chapter on the value of and how to maintain a daily journal of all activities that the wise sales person may regularly review to learn what is working and what is not. All of the top performers I knew kept one.

Shall I go on? Let us come to understand why the new sales mantra may well be: *question, listen, keep it simple, and make it yours.*

CHAPTER 1

Climate Change

In his article for The Business News Daily, entitled "Will Technology Advances Mark the Death of a Salesman?, senior writer Ned Smith writes "...observers speculate that advances in technology have made the traditional salesperson obsolete". While it is not hard to argue that the door to door sales person is today either an endangered species or extinct, it is generally acceptable that modern technology has reduced, substantially, the function of and/or need for a salesperson, "It's the old sales techniques themselves that have become obsolete because of trends that are reshaping the sales process." (again, Ned Smith, same article)

Pay attention to Ned, because he is smack on. But another aspect of the new technology is that the need for face to face communication and interactive selling is declining rapidly. And with that decline go person to person communication skills. Face to face selling is becoming an anachronism.

As of 2014, it was estimated that 42.3% of the global population can access the internet, and of those, some 80% have a smart phone. 93% of these smart phone owners use the device to make purchases. Where is the need for a sales person there? For the 0 and 1 counters, at present the digital explosion is some 3.2 zettabytes and is predicted to increase to 40 zettabytes of data in less than six years (one zettabyte is equal to one billion terobytes and that is a lot of 0's and 1's).

Simplified, an explosion akin to the first a-bomb times 100, squared. It is an in-comprehendible number. Today, large organizations can handle massive amounts of pertinent data regarding all things valuable to the sales process, but yet most companies examine only about 12%.

And buyers have similar access to such information. And what are they doing with it?

Control is now in the hands of the buyer. Buyers now provide each other with more brand information than before. They learn their needs for products and services, and, whether or not those products and services are needed in the first place. They have become digitally knowledgeable. Not only do they prefer not to interact with the sales person for information and post purchase follow up, they no longer need to.

The internet is rife with websites that make competitive product and service comparisons, formerly the purview of the sales person. In the auto industry alone, one cannot swing a cat without hitting a site that will tell the consumer what he or she should pay, not *expect* to pay, for a specific car in their geographical area, rendering the sales person unnecessary. Yesterday, a buyer had to hope for and or ask the sales person to provide the automobile's history; today, a website, for a price, will provide that information, which now the buyer expects from the sales person; arguably digital extortion.

Much of the present technology has kept the sales person from engaging initial face to face contact, from establishing confidence, from presenting competence, and from validating value and overcoming objections from real time, real world experience.

Why do I write this? Because anyone who has used the internet to research information for purchases, white papers, books, plans, work, and so forth, has to have come to the conclusion that while the internet may be considered an ocean of information, that ocean is littered with shoals and shallows. This implies that not all of the information found is accurate, true, or validated.

While an accomplished investigative reporter must have more than one source to validate the story, most people stop at the first site that provides what they want to read, not necessarily what they should read and that may not always be correct, ethical, or honest.

Along with the decline of face to face interaction and the progression of digital abbreviated messaging, "touch points" rather than good old human hands on real time "howdies", communication skills as basic as writing have fallen apart. The Los Angeles Times has recorded that industry loses billions due to poor writing. Think about that: how much credence and attention is given to a poorly written letter or email rife with abbreviations, misspellings, grammatical errors, and confusing text? If you cannot say what you mean, you will never mean what you say.

Inbound marketing and inside sales have increased exponentially as technology advances, again rendering previous sales methods and strategies obsolete. Who needs a sales person when one can conduct the entire transaction online? However, there is one truth in sales that is indestructible: people buy from people. And therein also lays the impact of the latest generations, clearly more cyber savvy than their predecessors they have, by default, changed the face of sales.

To the baby boomers, having it their way was critical and they had access to enough information to formulate what could and could not be done to satisfy their wants and needs. They could have face to face interaction with a sales person to communicate those wants and needs as desired for validation and negotiable pricing. Today, new buyers do not have to express person to person how they want things, since their needs can be satisfied their way by searching the internet. However, the accuracy and understanding of solutions that meet those needs may be questionable.

Technology can have another direct downside to the salesperson. Technology has made the salesperson accessible 24/7 and that is not such a good thing. All work and no play make Jane and Johnny dull and unproductive and, with this new accessibility, the sales person is expected to get more work done and faster than before. The expectation for increased productivity is growing.

Besides the noticeable increase in micromanagement that technology has created, there is also the concern that social media, in the workplace, may be used for more than just work. Statistics regarding how many times a day a person checks email, Facebook, Instagram, Twitter, and on and on make one wonder how any work gets done and how any face to face interactions take place at all. We have become distant and isolated (and sometimes less productive) in the glow of those small digital screens.

In her book "Talk to the Hand: The Utter Bloody Rudeness of the World Today, or Six Reasons to Stay Home and Bolt the Door" (that is a mouthful) Lynne Truss wrote in 2005 that as a society, "we are slouching into an age of social autism." She further writes that the new social technologies enable "limitless self-absorption" and begins an age of "hair-trigger sensitivity." (Rather explains the decline of civility in this country today.)

Clearly Ms. Truss does not see some effects of technology usage as helpful to the human condition or squeaky clean.

Is it?

Author Carolyn Stewart pronounced that social media... "encourages expectations for a custom-made reality and indignation about anything that deviates from our preferences."

As such media has begun to create "entitlement behaviors" for the digitally addicted population, how can one not expect the same from buyers?

Am I saying that technology is worthless and contributing to the dumbing down of America? Absolutely not. However, "abuse" and "over dependency" of any good thing is never prudent, especially when such eliminates jobs and the need for analytic thought.

However, technology has valuable benefits when properly considered and used: manual pen and paper work, such as endless reports, are now no longer necessary. Productivity and process tracking is no longer a bit by bit time consuming process, but recorded real time for real time evaluation. Data mining allows companies to finely target markets and such technology may reduce prospecting time substantially and literally obliterate the need for cold calling. Business now can reduce brick and mortar expense, as well as employees, either as no longer needed or not productive.

According to Ellen Ullman, writer and programmer, "One core tenet of Silicon Valley is that the ills caused by technology can be solved by the application of yet more technology." Which, to me and to anyone else with a concern for the future, is like saying that when someone throws a right hook punch at you, lean into it. Solving complicated problems with more complications does not make any sense and absolutely ignores the truth of the philosophy of Tao and the message of Occam's Razor.

Consider the statement made frequently in this book: "only a fool fights in a burning house."

While technology is supposedly grounded in the promise of complimenting and expediting man's endeavors, by its very purpose it continues to winnow down the necessity for human thought and labor.

Is that such a good thing? Not for those whose jobs have been replaced by a machine.

What has contributed more to the rising numbers of the unemployed: downturns in the economy, out-sourcing labor to other countries, or the explosion of technology designed to reduce the cost of whatever it replaces including reducing or eliminating jobs?

(Spoiler alert: all of the above.)

How far along the food chain of labor are the benefits generated by technology distributed? There is a fair measure of white and blue collar jobs that no longer exist.

One may consider here the difference between what is "right" and what is "good".

Has the technology explosion created more jobs for the common man? Relative to the subject of this book, what effects of technology may be capitalized on by the sales person?

There will always be the need for the sales person, beyond the need for a sales person to sell technology. There are buyers out there (and there will be more) that possess an innate distrust of doing business with a machine and technology that presents no intuitive or user-friendly obvious methods to respond to specific questions as well as guarantee satisfaction on a physical, organic level. Consider, however, that technology is in a constant state of flux and those issues, those objections, may soon be re-engineered to suit such consumers.

Sales people must re-examine present sales methods and processes to ensure continued loyalty of such buyers as well as spawn more through referrals. On broader terms, to include declining sales effectiveness of former methods as validated by studies highlighted in "The Sales Person's Index", the smart sales person must adjust methods to remain timely. The best way to do that is to return to basics and fundamentals to begin re-tuning what will work against the sterility and indifference of the machine.

Looking for opportunities to leverage the buyer's need for "accessibility" is one obvious path for today's sales person towards longevity. To provide consistent, experienced access to information as well as personalize the interaction is another method one may follow to retain value and viability.

The competition is not only the other guy's product, but now also technology, which is never neutral.

Given the extent of confusion in the world today, the pervasive epidemic of loss of trust and civility, is it any wonder that the sales person does not have the same value he or she once enjoyed? Perhaps the opportunity is ripe for the sales person to re-emerge as a necessary element in the core business formula. However, the return must begin from the very beginning of basics and fundamentals before timely, relative, and effective methods and processes to satisfy the new attitudes of today's "digital" customer can be enacted.

That may be accomplished by knowing one's stuff, knowing the competition, knowing existing and coming attitudes and trends, and understanding how, why, and what the customer thinks and responds to as well as what will drive the customer into (as well as away from) the cold arms of cyber-business.

It is no longer "only the strong survive"; longevity is achieved by working smart, thinking smart, and persevering.

All of this is not to suggest that business taken from the sales person and absorbed by technology may be recaptured, but that sales today can stand examination, effectiveness evaluation, change, and improvement to be viable.

But where is the hope for the sales person, the sales manager? Well, if one can understand that hope is a verb with its sleeves rolled up, some work will be required.

Knowing one's self, knowing how to take ownership of processes and methods, and having no fear to either accept or discard that which does or does not resonate will be the start of the work.

In Chapter 4 the point is made the methods described herein are not the only ones that may be effective. The sales person must follow those that make sense and stimulate an organic response.

It depends on you.

CHAPTER 2

The Sales Professional's Index

The following is the result of a lot of internet searching and the credit goes to the authors of numerous blogs and sites offering sales help and solutions on many levels. It should be remembered that while the internet is considered to be an ocean of information, parts of it are shoals two inches or less deep.

The point remains, however, that sales today is not perfect, nor are sales professionals, managers, and buyers and a process that is a combination of natural aptitude, science, and art is about as difficult to corral as it would be to herd cats. Sales is neither fish nor fowl but a simple process that is equally valuable to the buyer as it is to the sales person.

Use your own best judgment, but keep in mind the lessons that lurk behind the lines. Trust your gut.

Consider these statistics as you go through this book…

12.3% of all jobs are in sales, inside and out

1 Trillion dollars are spent annually on sales forces

55% of sales people should be doing something else other than sales

64% of sales people fail because they are in the wrong sales job

50% of sales managers admit they are too busy
to train or develop their sales force

50% of sales people have no planned approach

50% of sales professionals do not have a playbook

The win rate exceeds 50% for 66% of the companies
that have a defined sales process

Those with a playbook are 33% more likely to be high performers

The national sales closing rate is estimated to be 27%

67% of all sales people do not attain individual quota

27% of all companies do not even know if
their sales force has achieved quota

In any given situation, only 59% of the sales force is effective

65% of all sales calls end without the sales
professional asking for the order

65% of all sales calls are made to the wrong person

Replacing the bottom 20% of the sales force
relates to a 20% increase in productivity

Top performers out produce the average sales
person 2 -1; the below average 10-1

High performers are 25% better at qualifying

61% of sales people are good at uncovering customer
problems and are 28% more likely to achieve quota

Of sales people, 17% win less than 25%; 37% win less than 50%; 4% win more than 50%

20% of the sales force delivers 80% of the revenue

52% of sales professionals are able to access key players

46% of sales professionals believe their pipeline is accurate and spend 2.5 hours per week preparing forecasts

50% of a sales professional's results come from natural talent and aptitude

91% of buyers will offer referrals, but only 11% of sales professionals will ask for them

85% of sales people do not generate enough referrals

At 8 calls per hour it takes 6.25 hours to make 1 appointment

Only 2% of cold calls result in an appointment

40% of sales professionals experience serious unwillingness to make cold calls

92% of customer interactions take place by telephone

The average cost of customer contact by phone is $33.11, in person $276.48

Of phone calls, 82% of recipients remember tone versus what was said

82% of customers report being dissatisfied with telephone experiences

95% of all sales professionals talk too much

Buyers are 74% more likely to buy if they
perceive they are being listened to

A successful sales professional listens 75% of
the time and talks 25% of the time

First impressions are based 55% on looks,
38% sound, and 7% on what is said

Personality types and style aligned with the
prospect account for an 82% success rate

Buyers respond more favorably to personalization's

80% of sales are lost because of failure to
establish trust and credibility

A buyer values: competence 39%, quality of offering
21%, solution recommended 22%, price 18%

Only 14% of buyers consider price

65% of all buying decisions are emotionally based

70% of sales involve problem solving decisions;
30% of decisions are to gain something

Personal value has a 2 – 1 impact over business value

2% of sales result from the first meeting

50% of all sales go to the first contact

Average number of calls it takes to make a deal: 5

In getting to 5, 47% of sales professionals quit after
1 call, 22% after 2, 14% after 3, 12% after 4

8% of sales professionals ask for the order on the 5th call

2% of sales made on 1st contact, 3% 2nd, 5% 3rd, 10% 4th, 80% 5th-12th

Continuous training equates to 50% higher net sales per employee

On average a company loses 14% of its customers per year

Satisfying current customers is 3 – 10 times less
expensive than acquiring new ones

A 5% reduction in customer defection can lead
to as much as an 80% increase in profits

Customer relationship management improves
lead conversions by 300%

Customer relationship management applications
increase revenue up to 41% per sales person

Visuals are processed 60,000 times faster than text

After a presentation 64% remember stories
while only 5% remember statistics

Successful presentations contain 50% more objections

Satisfying objections leads to a 69% improvement in results

Lead nurturing leads 66% of buyers to respond with commitment

Nurtured leads result in 47% larger contracts

Inside recommendations account for an 82%
success rate; 20% from effective cold calls

Sales contributions to company strategy can lead
to a 15% increase in quota attainment

25% more revenue is achieved when sales and marketing are aligned

Companies of 100 – 500 employees have 7 or less decision makers

Buyers are moving away from industry publications

A brand is no longer what the company tells the customers
it is; it is what customers tell each other it is

"WE NEED TO STOP INTERRUPTING WHAT
PEOPLE ARE INTERESTED IN AND BE WHAT
PEOPLE ARE INTERESTED IN."
Craig Davis of J. Walter Thompson

CHAPTER 3

How to Use this Book...

(...or not to)

We learn by questioning. Little kids are great sales people because they are always asking "Why?" That is a great start and it is simple. Via the Dali Lama, we learned that Buddhist philosophy teaches to question everything: Siddhartha supposedly told his disciples to question everything, even what he taught them. The Socratic method of learning lies in asking questions. Christ advised his disciples to do the same. Today Pope Francis admonishes the faithful not to fear questioning. Even Albert Einstein spoke of the importance of questioning. Do not take anything at face value.

Here is another premise of this book: Occam's Razor. Know it? It states that in any given situation it is most likely the simplest solution or explanation is the best. With that consider another construct of the razor: don't over think the situation; be observant, and remove anything that does not make sense.

When questioning, keep it simple and have no fear or apprehension. The worst that can happen is "no" as a response. So what; move on. But never be hesitant about questioning as long as you are polite, direct, and to the point. Emotion has no place here (do not take it personally); however, "sales" for the prospect many times is emotional process, but "business" is not.

Give yourself credit for having a brain, despite all other influences to the contrary. I accept that you have one; use it. If you don't, this book won't work for you.

What you find following is the result of years of experience of not only myself but many others as well as observations of both good and bad across the continent.

What is presented herein worked for me and worked for the people I observed doing it. The question is, will it work for you?

That depends upon you. If you are seeking information to validate your decision to accept sales as a career, you will find straight forward "talk" to consider. If it makes sense to you, if it resonates, whether you have yet to start your career or have already started, then work to make it yours.

You can't do me any more than I can do you. See the chapter on "Making It Yours" to understand some methods you may employ to take ownership and put your stamp on what you have learned to do.

The internet is crowded with information about selling: how to techniques; psychology of selling; psychology of buyers; how to read body language to your advantage; consultant selling, solution selling, commodity selling, financial selling, prospecting, closing, qualifying, training, consultant services, and on and on and on. Find what you like, see if you can make it yours; if it resonates, try it.

To imply that the methods herein are the only ones that work would be the height of conceit and erroneously proselytizing. And I hate that.

There may be times when you are told "what" to do, rather than "how" to do it. Learning "how" is a better route than being told "what". If all you are hearing is "what" to do, find someone who will show you "how", otherwise, leave.

Look for a "mentor", someone in the organization who is willing to guide and help you through the early days and months of your career. Look for someone who is very good at what they do and has had a lot of time on the job; someone you feel confident can show you, or at least explain, "how".

Make your own decisions. But think first. Do homework, research, due diligence, until you are satisfied that the path you choose is the right one for you.

Don't fear failure. It is part of learning, an important part. Don't let failure stop your enthusiasm, your desires. A good leader will understand his failures as well as those of his followers and not begrudge or judge them for it.

Just don't stew over it or let failure become a habit.

Odds are that you will come across many people, both sales people and buyers, who are prone to saying "trust me" as a way to acceptance. You may take for granted that many buyers do not trust sales people for any number of reasons, some because of previous bad experiences, some because they lack confidence, some because they feel no resonance and make a negative decision based on first impressions. But trust is critical to success today, and continued success tomorrow.

Lincoln said that you can fool some of the people all of the time, and all of the people some of the time; Robin Williams said that you can fool some of the people all of the time and "abuse" the rest. But you can count on what goes around comes around; it is like a law of physics.

Take what you read within here, make it yours, and use it to your advantage. Or, consider all this and make your own educated decisions.

Trust me.

CHAPTER 4

Adjust, Adapt, Change

The sales person's role and responsibilities are no longer as simple and cut and dried as they were a couple of decades ago. It is a big wave to swallow and the smart money is on drinking it one glass at a time. This burden must be disassembled into workable pieces and that the sales person must be adept at employing all the technology and methodology at his or her disposal is critical if the job is to be accomplished successfully and with elegance and grace.

So what, in a few words, is this all about?

To be on top of his or her game, the sales person must have a command of the basics and fundamentals of the sales process and ownership of listening, questioning, negotiating, communicating, motivating, and managing skills.

Sales trainers from decades ago were fond of a technique of "reducing to the ridiculous", that is, to bring things down to the smallest common denominator. As complicated as the business world has become, the necessity to solve complicated problems with simple solutions is prudent. Knowledge of technology, products, industry, competition, trends, regulations, as well as inside and out of the customer and his or her company are critical.

The starting point has to be with ownership of basics and fundamentals, since backtracking when faced with an obstacle or roadblock to seek a simple solution does not a successful event make.

Keep in mind that 49% of companies have embraced e-commerce, both B2B and B2C. 59% of buyers prefer not to deal with sales people, 80% of the buying process will take place without any direct contact, and 93% of buyers choose to purchase on line.

Use your brain, think.

Be aware of changes in behavior and behavior trends.

Reduce customer dissatisfaction.

Adapt to new customer expectations.

Focus on profit realization instead of process automation.

Make the customer experience better, desirable. Make it frictionless.

Engage to make and maintain customer loyalty from the first contact.

Make the entire process transparent.

Work deliberately and frequently to increase customer retention.

Embrace customer preferences and understand how they came to be.

Personalize your presence, your offerings, and your pricing.

Leverage technology and data sources to differentiate you, your company, and your offering.

Return control of buyer education to yourself.

Focus on managing expectations, tolerating ambiguity, using judgment, shaping strategies and questions, and manage all the pieces: people, machines, and corporations.

An empathetic ability is necessary to understand and interpret data.

Work with technology; learn it, know it; understand the applications.

Respond quickly, but accurately, to opportunities.

Instead of pitching, have a conversation.

Recognize that now sales is a collaborative experience.

Employ technology to explore new leads and provide data to assist pre-qualifications.

Question, listen, keep it simple, and make it yours.

CHAPTER 5

The Seminal Salesperson

"What a piece of work is a man, how noble in reason, how infinite in faculties, in form and moving, how express and admirable, in action how like an angel, in apprehension how like a god! The beauty of the world, the paragon of animals." (Hamlet, Act 2 Scene 2)

Okay, sue me. I did spend a lot of time earning graduate and post graduate degrees in theatre.

"What a piece of work is a sales person, to work with people who many times defy reason, when having to master infinite skills and labors, including to think, act, speak, dance, and over all, perform well while endeavoring to present a form and image delightful, pleasing, and acceptable to the potential customer. Yes, an angel, a god, a conundrum." (John Fabiano)

Are good sales people born or are they nurtured and developed from observation, experience, training, curiosity, and imitation?

The question remains unanswered.

The high achievers I met "owned" every piece of what they were doing to bring in the business. Basics, fundamentals, always won out and it was hard to get away from that. Those who had turned their sales process into a Zen like state were the top performers. Those who knew the product and the competition backwards and forwards were top performers. Those who took the time to get to know their prospects inside and out were top performers. These were people who didn't compete with their clothes, grooming, and delivery. These were people who could deliver their presentations with their eyes closed, never having to look directly at the slide and who never "read" the slide, but talked from it.

And these top performers never seemed to be cold calling or hard prospecting; they always had several deals going at any given time. They were "in" the local business community, not "of" the local business community. They were established, known, and respected. And they made everything they did look effortless. While nobody is perfect, not even you or me, these folks came closer to perfection than anyone else. Everything was double, triple checked, verified, confirmed, and tested.

Was it easy? Of course not. It took time to reach such heights; experience that came from mistakes learned hard or easy; getting up and dusting off while coming to understand the lesson. We learn from failure. But they put the time in to "own" all of it, and to make sure it came across naturally, they put the time in to make it all theirs. Yes, one could watch and learn from them, but no one could ever "do" them. 90% of creativity is theft and it works only when one makes it his or her own.

Sales is a craft to be learned and if it was easy, everyone would be doing it and you never would have purchased this book. Attend: *a master baker does not start at the top of his profession. A father in law, many years ago, had me work in his bakery for a year as payment for permission to marry his daughter. He was Czech and in any European country, a master baker is an artist. In the old days, the novice started out doing menial jobs at the baker's farm. After several years of shoveling you know what, he moved to the actual bakery, where he started with inside menial jobs, and then to the most basic things: lugging sacks of flour, cracking eggs, shelving product that needed to rise in retarders, sweeping floors and cleaning work benches. Then if he did that well enough, he was introduced to "bench work" making bagels, cookies,* pastries, and the like. There were many steps he had to learn before he got to the top, which was a decorator—that took skill and creativity and was an artist's work. It would take a young man 10 to 15 years, pending how hard he worked and his skill and aptitude, before he advanced to the decorators' bench. I was artistic, worked hard, and had the aptitude, and as the son-in-law and heir apparent, it took me about two months.

I advanced quickly because I learned quickly. I knew my stuff.

As a sales engineer starting out with a leading telecommunications company, I had a sales manager who didn't really fit the profile. A white guy who wore his hair in an afro, liked to drink his lunches at a topless bar, and belonged to a photographic club that once a month would hire nude models. He was very well groomed and wore only the finest, classic suits, shirts, and ties. He was an excellent listener and successful at his job. He was extremely street smart. He relied on me for almost all of his product knowledge and I developed a great deal of respect for him; he was never judgmental. And, for whatever reason, I was his favorite in the office. One day, as he enjoyed his vodka lunch at his favorite "peeler" bar, he questioned me about what I thought of the capabilities of the sales people I frequently accompanied on calls. As the office was relatively new and the company was just a few years after lifting off, sales were not robust, but enough to encourage further investment. As one might expect, the 80-20 rule, ruled: 20% of the sales people brought in 80% of the business. "Why do you suppose our one salesman closes the most and the other four struggle?" He asked. "Because da cats in da know ain't bustin' dey hump" he exclaimed before I could answer.

Nailed it. Right there. In ten words. Simple.

Our top sales person made it look effortless because he had put a great deal of effort into making sure he knew more about the product than anyone else, that he knew the market better than anyone else, that he knew more about his prospect and his prospect's business than the prospect did, and he knew what sales techniques worked where and when. He knew when to get aggressive and when to walk away. He always outperformed everybody else and always surpassed quota. And he never stopped learning.

You couldn't beat this guy even if you were giving the product away.

He knew how to distinguish himself above all others in the market, the field, the community, and the office. He knew exactly what he needed to know, top to bottom, and, above all, was able to lead a pleasant, leisurely, family life outside of work. He wasn't "bustin' his hump".

Words to remember, maybe even worthy of a tattoo: Work smart.

Quality #1: A sales person absolutely, positively, always must be an exceptionally good listener. Most folks are in an accepting mode when they come to believe that what they are saying is heard. A national statistic reports that 95% of all sales people talk too much. A good sales person listens 75% of the time talks 25% of the time.

We learn by listening and a good sales person knows that almost all of the time a prospect will reveal how he or she can be closed if the sales person listens carefully.

The prospect really isn't that concerned about how much the sales person knows about the product but he or she is absolutely concerned about how the situation, the problem, may be solved.

Let the prospect talk, and the sales person learns a lot, first, as to whether or not this is qualified prospect. Is this the right person to be proposing? Who is the decision-maker? What is the problem? How does the prospect see the solution—something that makes him/her look good, something absolutely necessary, something that resolves a business need, or something that satisfies an emotional need? Does the prospect understand what is being said? Will the product, solution, application, service, effectively solve the problem? And a great deal more.

Quality #2: A sales person is prepared to do whatever needs doing to secure the order. The sales person is energized by success. He/she works long hours to get started building a fecund pipeline, learn the product, know the competition, understand his prospects, and how to improve his sales collaboration process and skills.

Quality #3: A sales person is not only unafraid of hard work, but looks forward to it, thrives on it. See #2, again. Sales is not a 9 to 5 job and requires alertness at all times. One never knows where the next prospect and opportunity may come from.

Quality #4: A sales person is exactingly thorough for the purposes of excellence and perfection in all that he or she does. No stone is left unturned; meetings and presentations are reviewed and rehearsed until both are elegant, effortless, and in anticipation of questions and objections. A sales person rarely asks a leading question of which he does not already know the answer. He/she anticipates the prospects questions, objections, and moves. Want to achieve something close to perfection right away? "Stop doing that non-excellent stuff now." (T. Watson)

Quality #5: A sales person is personable, which is to say to him/her, a stranger is a friend yet to be known. He/she has an ability to be comfortable and capable around people and make them comfortable and unguarded in his or her presence. He/she can be chameleon-like, knowing that prospects respond to people of the same style and type. Seeing the prospect crumbling his cornbread over his greens, the comfortable sales person will do the same thing. "Oh man, I thought I was the only one who did that. Good, isn't it?" You betcha, scooter.

Quality #6: A sales person is well groomed; not necessarily a dandy or a fashionista, but possessed of quality, well-tailored, clean, and conservative clothes, polished shoes and modest accessories and jewelry. Well groomed, no tattoo's showing, good breath, either clean shaven or well-trimmed. Non-threatening and welcoming in appearance to the average man on the street.

Quality #7: A sales person has a pleasant voice without an overshadowing accent. Studies have shown that a prospect will remember tone over what is said. Speech should be natural and effortless and not mimicking the prospect's accent, which sometimes is hard to avoid.

Quality #8: A sales person is a quick study, who can pick up on things and use them to his/her advantage in a short time. He/she is aware of visual as well as audible cues the prospect puts out. Learn to understand body language. Sherlock Holmes' strength was his high degree of observation.

Quality #9: A sales person is patient, very patient. He/she also understands that the early bird gets the worm: 50% of sales go to the first contact. Nobody likes to be pushed, especially by a sales person. Patience and waiting will sometimes triumph when all else has failed. Remember "fools rush in…"? Be patient and let the other guy make a fool of himself while you watch for and capitalize on his mistakes

Quality #10: A sales person is an advocate for his prospect, his point of contact, his company. Advocacy breeds loyalty. He/she will fight for his prospect and contact's needs both in his/her company and that of the contact.

Quality #11: A sales person is openly altruistic. He/she is always looking to help his prospect and customers.

Quality #12: A sales person is sincerely empathetic. Sincerity makes up for a lot of sins and empathy is morally and ethically correct behavior. Someone who genuinely cares will stand above the crowd.

Quality #13: A sales person is truthful always. Wicked ways come back to haunt and what goes around comes around. Sooner or later, the big one will come crashing down. Success will elude forever. Not letting the truth stand in the way of a good presentation is a recipe for slow death.

Quality #15: A sales person possesses a healthy, balanced ego; he/she has solid, high self-esteem but is never conceited or condescending. Confidence is critical; the sales person must believe in himself/herself.

Quality #16: A sales person is never satisfied with his/her present performance; among other things, he is always interested in improving his training, education, and how to advance his position. Like a shark, a good sales person has to keep moving to survive.

Quality #17: A sales person has the drive and will to succeed. This goes to confidence: having the will means continuing with the plan as created and not slowing down or walking away at the first sign of obstacles or surprises. Reward rarely comes without risk, but if you know your stuff, you can hedge your bet and have the odds in your favor. Following through to the end is "having the will". No fear.

Quality #18: A sales person plans his work and works his plan. He/she works smart. Pretty simple. It goes without saying that a sales person must be goal setter, goal oriented and, he/she must have the will to see things through.

Quality #19: A sales person will find at least 50% of sales will come from natural talent and aptitude. And herein is a good point from which to make a decision, especially regarding aptitude: don't like ringing doorbells or calling strangers? Don't go into sales.

Qualities for success and survival that were part of a seminar I delivered in the 90's: (Still resonant today.)

1. Believe in yourself; know yourself; like yourself
2. Believe in your products and company
3. Believe in your customers; be an advocate
4. Unconditional loyalty to your managers; make partners, mentors
5. Manage your managers; be two steps ahead; ask questions
6. Unconditional loyalty to your customers; make partners

7. Manage your customers, be four steps ahead; ask questions and shut up and listen
8. Communicate well with customers and company
9. Be self-motivating, self-starting
10. Take reality pills daily
11. Discipline, plan, discipline, repeat
12. Practice the basics and don't lose sight of the mission
13. Know when to hold 'em; know when to fold 'em
14. Make time for yourself and your family."

"There is no effort without error and short coming." Teddy Roosevelt It adds up to a lot, but it is all achievable with solid work, effort, and desire.

CHAPTER 6

The Right Sales Job

If you cannot think of any product or service that needs not to be sold, then you will come to understand that there are not many companies and firms that do not require a sales force.

However, there remain today many companies that are in business despite themselves and of those, many rely completely and absolutely on the sales force to keep them alive. These, to be kind, are not the best places to look for sales work; think of boiler rooms and sweat shops. Many smaller companies and firms hire younger, inexperienced people with the purpose being to get them to sell to their family and friends while carrying out other functions at their own expense and all the while, working on commission only (the ancient standard door to door vacuum sales model and most door to door sales companies). Running out of family and referrals or just not being trained enough to understand the referral process, is a ticket out the door as there are more potential hires around and the company endeavors to make as little investment in the sales force as possible.

There are other companies that remain anachronisms and are led and managed by those who, for whatever reason, have not been able to change with the times leaving the sales force to scrape by when up to date methods and better treatment of them would produce significantly better results and substantially more loyal employees.

But let's make things simple, as that is one of the main tenets of this book. You should know by now who and what you are and you should never jump at the first sales opportunity without careful considerations. In fact, it is prudent to practice your interviewing skills on companies that don't really interest you; there is no substitute for practice and the experience gained; you want to be as confident as you possibly can be.

Remember, some 55% of the sales people out there shouldn't be in sales at all and 64% are in the wrong sales job. Good sales people are not statistics, but stand outs and possess a strong, balanced, healthy ego.

As with Jeff Foxworthy's "You know you are a redneck…" consider the following as, "You know you are in the wrong job…(if or when)"

…Your sales management insists you only talk to the president of the prospect company.

…You must learn and deliver the sales pitch and accompanying scripts verbatim without deviation.

…You must spend several hours a week, usually after normal business hours to, make telephone cold calls.

…You are expected to cold call by knocking on strangers' doors.

…Your comp plan is commission only from day one.

…You are expected to start cold calling on day one.

…You have no playbook.

…You have no training schedule.

…Your training is limited to product only and has nothing about a sales process relative to the product or network selling and inbound marketing.

…Your sales manager tells you what to do rather than showing you how to do it.

…Your sales manager does not attend your sales calls.

…You are micromanaged.

…Your forecast report takes more than an hour complete.

…You have to pay for your own sales materials and kits.

…You realize you have forgotten more than your sales manager knows.

…You just do not mesh or like not only the sales manager but also the support staff.

Any one of these should set off alarm bells and tell you to get out now. You are not going to make it there nor will you learn anything new other than it is a place where you do not want to be.

As you will learn how to nurture prospects and accounts, you too, must be nurtured since success does not happen overnight and a rose without water and care does not blossom.

So, what kind of company are you looking for? First of all, it must be selling a product or service that resonates with you, is something that you like as well, and of which you have at least a moderate understanding.

Do your due diligence, your homework, your research. There are many places on the net to search for reviews and evaluations of the company AND the management and executive staff. Find out what kind of financial condition the company is in. Research the comp plans and benefits programs. Determine through your homework what the future holds for that product or service. Has the company been growing or shrinking? What do its customers have to say about the company, its offerings, and its sales and service people? What do existing employees say about their company?

First impressions work both ways; assuming you know how to make a good first impression, how is that of the company personal you first meet? Are they like you? Do the offices look professional, organized, well-lit and clean? Is the paint on the walls peeling? Is personal hygiene and grooming questionable? Do these people talk as professionals? Do they keep talking and rarely let you get a word in? Do they ask you questions but don't give you a chance to answer them? Are they confrontational or fawning or direct and confident?

Simply put, do you like them at first glance and pass? An old sales chestnut states that you will never sell people you do not like. Consequently, you have to like the people you work with.

This is no small matter: this is your life and, be warned, there are, unfortunately, any number of unscrupulous companies that have absolutely no compunction about taking advantage of you and have no intention of maintaining any sort of covenant or loyalty with you.

What follows is a simple exercise a fledgling sales person (or any sales person who has not done this before and wants to know if it is worth it). This is a simple Excel program; it is an inventory of financial needs and a projection of potential income. It isn't that difficult to figure out if one knows basic Excel and allows one to determine if the job is worth it and how.

Do this before you say "yes" to the job. Make a sound decision based on data and fact. First calculate your monthly expenses and desired disposable income for entertainment and other, non-necessary things. Be brutally honest with yourself.

Now calculate your estimated income, at quota. What is your monthly salary, if at all? What is your commission or leverage rate? What is your monthly quota? What is the average size contract in dollars? How many contracts does it take to reach quota? What is your closing ratio? (one out of three, one out of four, one out of five or more?) Multiply the number of contracts to reach quota by the closing ratio to determine how many prospects you will need. How long does it take for a deal to mature to contract, on average? How many deals can you realistically manage a month? What would be your commission at quota? Plus salary, what then would your total income be at quota? Where does that leave you versus your monthly expenses? Upon evaluation, do you have the time and skills to achieve the monthly quota? If there is a negative delta between income and expenses, how many more contracts would be needed? And how does that fit with your time to prospect and manage that many deals at your closing ratio?

PERSONAL MONTHLY EXPENSES VS MONTHLY INCOME INVENTORY

MONTHLY EXPENSES		MONTHLY INCOME	
Mortgage/Rent	$1,000	Quota	$40,000
Gas	$50	Commission %	3.50%
Electric	$275	Commission @ Quota	$1,400
Water	$50	Salary	$1,500
Cable	$110	Average Contract $$	$4,000
Wireless	$25	Closing Ratio	25%
Cell(s)	$100	Contracts To Meet Quota	10
Internet	$65	Sales Cycle (Weeks)	2
Land Line	$40	Proposal Load/Week	5
Trash	$30	Proposals Required	40
Home Insurance	$50	Cumulative Rq'd Time (Weeks)	80
Car Payment(s)	$259	Proposals/Week (@4.3 weeks)	17
Car Insurance	$85	Proposals/Long-Short	-12
Parking	$0	MONTHLY TOTAL INCOME	$2,900
Laundry	$40	MONTHLY TOTAL EXPENSES	$3,669
Maintenance	$90	DELTA	$769
Grocery	$500		
Credit Card Debt	$400		
Other Loans/Debt	$0		
Other Expenses	$200		
Disposable Income	$300		
MONTHLY TOTAL	$3,669.00		

The hard decisions come down to determining how long it takes you to close a deal and bring in a contract from prospecting to closing. Estimate based on your best and honest feelings about your abilities relative to those actual cycle times learned from experienced sales people in the office. It will take a while to calculate something close to reality, but if you keep a journal of all of your daily sales efforts, it will come.

Start out with a closing ratio of one out of four (25%) as that is estimated to be a national average. If you are not comfortable, start with a lower percentage. Keep a journal of your activities and calendars to make effective determinations. Consider demands on your time as well. If getting to your goals or just breaking even appears to take more time than you have with all of your responsibilities and desires, red flags should be appearing and you need to re-evaluate the time the job demands and if you can afford to re-arrange your personal time demands.

Remember, sales is not a 9 to 5 job and if you are led to believe that it is, you are not getting the whole story.

Make every effort to talk with current employees, preferably in private, in order to overcome inhibitions. A key question is how long does it take to get to the first year's income as quoted in the job description or by the interviewer. Sales at target does not happen overnight; experience is needed to make it happen and make it consistent. Avoid "pie in the sky" compensation declarations; if it sounds too good to be true, it probably isn't true.

There are sales people that work strictly on commission only and for some, that is the only way they want it. Generally, commission only translates to a higher commission percentage than salary plus commission (also called "leverage") as salary is not included and the plan is pay for performance. But how much must you sell to reach what a commission plus salary monthly income would be?

Accepting a sales position in a new industry or city for commission only is not a wise idea unless you can afford to live for several months without a regular income. Everybody does not hit the ground running and performing to plan. Time is required to develop prospects to buyers to contracts and, chances are, time may outstrip what money you have put aside to see you through until your goals are within close reach. Some companies will provide a short term salary for "x" number of weeks to help you get started. Here is where your homework saves you from hard times as you can compare how long YOU think it will take you to get there to what your prospective employer says it will. It has been my experience that few companies offer enough paid time to make sense. Some companies will offer this start up salary as "recoverable" meaning that what has been paid to you during this period you will pay back to the company from your commissions. What happens when the draw starts to accumulate to more than your sales bring in commissions? You won't last very long being in the hole.

Be cautious, do your homework, and hold onto your trust as you take a daily "reality pill"

To further help you in deciding if you want a career in sales or want to continue in sales…"here's a quick test to help you evaluate yourself as a sales professional. Answer either yes or no to each of the following 10 questions."

1. Do I learn as much as I can about my prospects before I call (particularly why they should buy what I sell)?
2. Do I start each interview by discussing something I know interests my prospects?
3. Do I start a compete presentation with the benefits I can offer and their significance to my prospect?
4. Do I ask questions to be sure my prospect understands and appreciates the benefits I offer?
5. When my prospect makes an objection, do I listen respectfully, restate it, and then answer it before I go on with my presentation?
6. Do I anticipate possible price objections by explaining value and stressing quality?
7. Do I build confidence by telling my prospect names of some of our well-known customers and how satisfied they are?
8. Do I emphasize the service I will give when my customer buys?

9. Do I sell through the eye as well as the ear: do I use all the selling aids available to me?
10. Do I emphasize benefits, value, and service when I close to make it easier for my prospect to say yes than to say no?

To score, multiply the number of your "no" answers by 10, then subtract that number from 100."
(Source: Professional Sales Manual, National Sales Development Institute)

POST SCRIPT: It is an excellent idea to keep a daily journal of activities and results for each deal in process. Analyze for deal lengths, closing ratios, diverse industry effects, and, ultimately, what works and what doesn't. Review your past efforts frequently to learn from them.

CHAPTER 7

Step 0

There are pages and pages of websites talking about how to set quotas and why each particular method is the best. It is a quota jungle out there that the wise executive knows he has to understand if it is worth it before heading off on safari.

Before a business can get to the point where business process validation, improvements, creations, etc. are implemented, it has to have BUSINESS first and therein lies the value of "management to the business". It is "Step 0" in building a successful sales force.

What is glaringly missing is a process to actually validate if there is achievable business capable of making the entire enterprise worthwhile. While it is one thing to do research to determine how fecund the existing market is, it is another thing to determine if the company can extract enough business from that market with the present plans and sales force to stay alive.

Existing companies need to apply this thinking to help and validate realistic targets and quotas.

Pundits talk of seasonal influences, market trends, competition, territory divisions, varying quotas for diverse performers, and a host of other subjects that completely leave out the sales professional.

All of the executive planning to make a profit is well and good, but with the human resources and market available, if the sales force, due to skills, timing, numbers, and strength, can't do it, what is the point of creating arbitrary, subjective quotas that are meaningless, not validated, and undoable?

How does one go about determining what is "doable"

1. Does sufficient market exist in the given ground where the company plays?
2. Who owns what percentages of the market and why?
3. What length of life span does the product have, if one at all?
4. What is the consistently average closing ratio of the sales force?
5. What is the consistently effective length of the sales cycle from prospect to close?
6. How many proposals can an individual sales person effectively handle at one time?
7. What historic data exists regarding previous years' new sales, aftermarket sales, and annual lost customers?
8. How has training affected performance?

These are simple, basic considerations that must be answered before a company can begin to plan for success, measure success, and motivate the sales force to maximum performance.

And, to insure success with this plan, this "Step 0", the following should be invoked:

1. The process must be simple
2. The process must be fluid, and capable of elegant change
3. The sales force must have at least some ownership in the process
4. The executive staff must have the will to carry the plan through its life cycle, regardless of when goals are achieved

Once the process, a formula, is in place, the company can then determine how much market needs to be secured by:

1. Improving the closing ratio
2. Decreasing the sales cycle
3. Increasing the sales force
4. Improving prospecting and lead quality
5. Implementing/increasing sales training
6. Finding/creating more market

There is a maxim that Gene Roddenberry put into a "Star Trek" script: "Only a fool fights in a burning house." Indonesians refer to the unattainable as "water of the moon", something that simply does not exist. Acting without fact is like attempting to find "water of the moon" or "fighting in a burning house", something with negative consequences for both parties.

That is why "Step 0" is so important.

And, despite the swamp of technology that mires us all today, the smart money is on the KISS principle: "Keep it simple, stupid"

In computer parlance, zero precedes one, so therein "0" is the actual beginning, not "1" as generally perceived.

The success of any venture depends upon a plan and a plan must begin with an understanding of the facts, the ground, the environment, the position, what is out there, and as a result of careful examination and comparison, a determination of what is required to achieve success and more critical, if the effort will be profitable.

A successful business will start with a sound, full blown, business plan and critical to such are the market demographics: how many/much of the target market exists?

So it would precede that a clear, concise definition of the product's/ service's value proposition is necessary. For example, in the funeral business, today the prime target is the baby boomer: age range is right, money is right, attitude and thinking are closely aligned, among other factors. At issue is if there are enough boomer buyers in the territory to sustain the profitability targets and does the existing sales force demonstrate the skills and a success ratio to secure the required business. Given such totals in the area and the existing sales force and its skills (cycle time, closing ratio, etc.) it is possible to establish a base line of probability for success and subsequent targeted profitability.

But yet, many sales organizations begin with an arbitrary number determined to represent the specific target multiplied by profit margin and calculated with overhead expenses. The sales person is assigned a quota that is his or her share of that number divided by the number of sales people employed.

According to Paul DiModica, a sales process pundit, several non-functional methods include some rather arbitrary and subjective processes that have little or nothing to do with the reality of the entire picture. Sales people may be charged with a quota that was their performance at plan last year plus "x" percent or an imaginary number sold to the sales person as income potential at plan or what the trade press says the industry will bear in the coming year; and other questionable methodology.

Tao speaks to natural simplicity and naturalness of non-interference with the natural course of things. So, that in mind, it makes sense to start with who, what, where, when, why, how, with what, and how long. Simple.

Given the geographic location, does the value proposition of the product make sense? Many years ago I was teaching at a small parochial school in a rural part of New York State. The closest city was Albany and that was some 3 hours south. The general population was either farmers or mill workers and few had attended college. I was pitched a brand new religious education curriculum that spoke to all things one would encounter in an urban environment; it had an extreme Rod McKuen flavor to it, plenty of clever graphics and photos, and a whole lot of other pieces for which my students had no frame of reference.

Somebody did not think about the viability of the product for that market and it would be waste of money, time, and, in this case, would serve to confuse my students. I made sure every student had access to the Old and New Testaments (knowing full well that in this area, all had at least one copy of each at home) and built my lesson plans around that. These were good, God-fearing people who believed in the unencumbered simplicity of the Word and they knew of the Word and were comfortable with it.

I knew my "market" and delivered to it. The curriculum company had not done its homework and was in the wrong market.

It is called managing to the business.

And, try as one might, the concept that if you can't measure it, you can't manage it is inescapable.

Assuming the value proposition is in place and a target customer has been established, now, how many are out there? Of the gross totals, specifically, how many of these targets exist within a reasonable range of space and time? The formulation of the target includes need, desire, money, and motivation, the strength of all of which will figure into the complexity, density and duration of the sales process and cycle.

Does a sales force exist that is up to the task? Can one be hired that is capable of achieving the desired success? National averages indicate that an approximate 25% closing ratio is pervasive so unless more specific, validated information exists it makes sense to start there. What that means is that for each sale, there have to be four proposals: one will go to contract, three will not.

How long is the average sales cycle? National averages report a five call process, but that cannot accurately represent specific industry and sales cycles. When I managed a capital sales operation, a sale could take anywhere from three months to three years, all dependent on complexity, size, and cost. Only those experienced in the industry/ product (and through personal experience) can determine the cycle length as well (and this is important, too) the number of proposals an average sales person may be expected to effectively manage at any given time.

So, the formula involves the available number of possible prospects and how many prospects are needed to be closed for one sale, how long it takes to get a contract, and how many sales people are available to accomplish the number.

A sales person has an average closing ratio of one out of four, his territory shows some 100 possible prospects, or 25 potential contracts. But how many proposals can that sales person effectively manage each week, month, quarter? How does that work out for the entire sales force?

Taken all together, "Step 0" will help determine if the entire event is worth it and what sales performance is required to achieve results desired and beyond.

The market and sales force has to be understood fully and confidence in performance is paramount.

It's called "fishing" not "catching". And therein lays the allure, the mystery, the skill, and the desire to learn fishing basics and how to fish.

As with anything worthwhile, it takes time, experience, knowledge, research, homework...and a lot of other serious endeavors.

So much of the natural world controls optimum "fishing" conditions: time of the year, time of day, moon phases, tides, temperatures (air and water), salinity, surface conditions, winds, wind direction, water depth, water visibility, food source (bait) availability, oxygen levels, and a host of other conditions over which man has absolutely no control.

And, if that is not enough, there is the necessary equipment, aka "tackle" dictated by 100's of different sources, "experts" and the industrial fishing combine. Consider the variety of rods, reels, lines, leaders, lures, weights, jigs, hooks, crank baits, sinking lures, swimming lures, plastics, live bait, dead bait, outriggers, down riggers, kite riggers, teasers, chum (real and artificial) ...and on and on and on.

I started fishing at an early age, in a town wherein if you could not bait your own hook by the time you were 4 you were banished to some place inland and without a body of water and clear horizon. Throughout my career in sales I was always struck by the comparison.

It's called "selling" not "order taking". And therein lays the necessity for understanding the product, service, market, prospect, and buyer as well as the current industry status quo and revealing trends.

As with anything worthwhile, it takes time, experience, knowledge, research, homework…and a lot of other serious endeavors.

So much of the "real" world controls optimum buying conditions: time of year; particular quarter; "C" level attitudes (from "E" through "F" and "I" to "O"); decision processes and cycles; pro and con boards; attitudes and personalities of influencers and decision makers; stern defenders of the status quo and their own reputations; cognizance of problems and solutions; acceptance of extent technology; and the list goes on and on.

To consistently turn sales efforts into orders, it is necessary to have a plan, a process, and talented sales people, as well as an inclusive, but simple to understand, playbook for the entire sales process and cycle, covering as many scenarios as possible.

All of which may explain the plethora of "business process" consultants and web companies clogging Google today.

Studies have shown over 55% of people in sales should be doing something else other than sales. 20% of the sales force generates 80% of the volume; a good sales person has natural talent and aptitude, is a good listener, and exudes competence. 67% of today's sales force does not attain quota. The current national sales closing ratio, on average, is between 25% to 27%.

Studies have also shown that folks remember stories better than statistics, but no one ever increased profitability from the lessons of Poe's "Cask of Amontillado". Down in the dirt, it is confirmed, validated facts that make the difference. And, like it or not, facts and numbers are pretty much the same.

So, what do these stats tell us? Current sales is not efficient and not providing an equitable return.

And how do we change that?

Are the expectations placed on the sales force realistic?

Managing to the business requires a flexible and liquid process to examine the market, the sales force's performance statistics, existing sales process, past sales, planned/proposed sales, and profitability goals.

And why? What is the value to the company?

Increased profitability, increased business, efficiency improvement, expedited and improved planning, effective employee usage and management, effective and specific targeted management and marketing. It can open the tunnel wider so one can see the surroundings beyond the light at the end.

Working smart begins with planning smart.

By doing this, the company can determine if "it" is there, which is to say the ultimate goal(s) of the company. After all is said and done, is "it" worth all the effort, expense, and sturm und drang? Are arbitrary and subjective targets realistic? Is the status quo successful; is the process(s) working? Is the present "doctrine" effective? What is broken and what is not becomes visible.

Now, one can wade through the internet (after all, the internet is an ocean of information, but the wise have learned that most of it is only 2 inches deep) searching for the right company with the right cost effective plan for accomplishing goals or, one can look within the company and the inherent experience and wisdom of the employees. Do the latter first.

Studies have produced data that indicates aligned sales and marketing reach to 25% more revenue. Sales contributions to company strategy creation lead to a 15% increase in quota achievement. Companies that foster sales "ownership" of strategy and process historically do better than those who do not.

So how does one begin?

Several things can be working at the same time. First, however, is the creation of a specific, accurate, and universal value proposition: why does the market need the product, the service and how will it benefit the customer?

Next, determine the available market.

In the telecommunications industry we knew every company needed a system, but of what size and how many had systems at the end of life cycles/ROI and/or in need of upgrading or expanding? To that end, the market was divided by product sizing and then researched to understand that the average life cycle was 5 years, meaning that, as a median assumption, 20% of the market place was in play at any time. From that, data was established as to how many prospects of each size system were potential, qualified customers.

Average cost per system may be prepared using current data and may be extended via assumptions regarding future increases.

Understanding the existing sales cycle now becomes important. What is the average closing ratio? What is the length of the average sales cycle? At any given time, how many opportunities can the average sales rep effectively manage towards closure?

Previous after-market sales history needs to be evaluated for average annual growth or decline and included in the mix. How and by whom that business is brought home is also to be researched.

As an example: the average retail price of the product is $250,000. Of a market of 2000, at a 5 year (or 20%) life cycle, 400 are potential prospects. With a closing rate of one out of four (25%), it may be anticipated that 100 will come to contract, bringing the total annual anticipated revenue to $25,000,000. If the average proposal sales cycle (from prospect to close) is 2 months, and the average sales rep can carry 4 proposals at any given time, which equals an annual proposal load expectation per rep of 24. At the 25% closing ratio, 6 proposals will be brought to contract. With an average retail price of $250,000, anticipated performance for a sales rep would be $1,500,000, which, when divided into the anticipated annual revenue equates to a sales force of 16.6, or 17 sales reps.

Got the idea?

See Appendix One for an example, simplified worksheet of Step 0 that follows the above description.

As any well-constructed Excel program is fluid, "what if's" may be calculated simply.

In the Appendix One example, Column F shows the results if the closing ratio is increased to 30% and the proposal cycle time is reduced to one month instead of two. Notice that it increases anticipated annual sales revenue by $5 million, increases rep annual production to $3 million, doubles annual closed proposals per rep, but requires 7 less sales representatives.

For companies with multiple territories, this program may be expanded for each and cumulative totals pulled from the appropriate calculations.

At a 25% closing ratio, with 6.25 hours required to get one appointment, at 8 calls per hour (a recognized universal average), each rep will need to spend 25 hours per week cold calling to get at least 4 prospects of which one will close. That is just about 50% of the week that would be put to better use given the return on time spent. Never forget how valuable a resource time is to a sales person.

But what about the after-market business? Assume, for example, that such accounts for 33% of the total revenue or $8.25million added back in. History has shown that for this company (as example), this business increases 8.5% annually, so this year's expectation is $8,951,250. How is that target met? How will it be met and at what cost may be estimated at a 33% new business growth.

Profit determination can be as simple as holding the line at a specific percentage of goods sold and deducting overhead and all operating costs.

And all this calculated from an Excel program that, very probably, you and your company have more than adequate talent to produce.

And including sales employees in this process ensures a sense of ownership, which, again and again, has proven to be a technique that returns better results than pushing down plans and processes from above without sales force input.

A simple Excel "Step 0" may be found in Appendix Two. This worksheet is for a simple operation. In the case of the example shown, how many reps are mathematically required to achieve the monthly quota.

Another valuable aspect of this worksheet is that it calculates prospecting time using national averages of calls per hour and hours required to secure one appointment. This is to allow the user to determine if the prospect method employed (here cold calling) is an effective use of time as it shows the percentage of selling time left after prospecting time.

A closing ratio is with regards to proposals; it is not representative of appointments scheduled. Some appointments can lead to unqualified prospects or, for what other reasons just do not make it to proposal stage. At an arbitrary number, consider an appointment to proposal ratio of 25%, although it may be quite higher than that. Quality prospecting reduces that. Do not think every appointment leads to a proposal, much less a closed deal.

This does provide a lot of mathematically correct data that can be used to determine "what if's" and "how to's". If either math's out short of target, then try changing cycle time, closing ratios, and prospecting time. Regardless, remember the premise: make it yours.

With a little imagination and a basic understanding of this simple program, you may be able to expand it to provide information by territory, product sizes, average system costs, and so on to help you get to the same result: How many sales reps are required, given current circumstances, what is a reasonable quota for each, and, what may the company expect in total revenue.

It is simple Excel programing and in changing what you see to your benefit, to make it yours, if it doesn't fit your needs, is encouraged. However, the basic concepts remain.

CHAPTER 8

Rating Sales Calls

A good sales person understands where the sales process is at any time. He further qualifies in many ways during each sales call.

Sales is all about numbers; numbers take time to accumulate; time wasted is time lost that might well have been better spent on a qualified prospect.

Qualify at every call, in person or by phone. Don't know what to do or say next? Close, ask for the order which is just another method of qualifying.

But how do you rate sales calls? How do you know which works better than others? How good should you feel about the opportunity following each call? How can you continue to plan your work as well as be fluid if you do not know where you stand with the prospect?

If, when returning from a sales call, you do not know where you are or how you feel about the call or whether or not this is a qualified opportunity, then it probably isn't. You have to make the most of each call.

There should be an exact plan for each call. What is the purpose of the call? What should be accomplished? How is that to be accomplished?

What questions should be asked? What questions will the prospect ask? What objections will appear? How will objections be overcome? How do I improve my relationship with the prospect? How do I establish trust? Can I accomplish all I need to do in the time allotted?

If anything, plan out the call. Rehearse the plan. Be exhaustive; think; think again. Work smart.

If going in for a big presentation, make sure you know exactly what the prospect wants to hear and what you need to say. Be economical with your words: an old show business maxim is "less is more". Also, remember "KISS" keep it simple, stupid. Not that your prospect is dumb (don't ever let the prospect feel that) but the more complicated things get, the more there are chances for things to go wrong and you need to work hard, in advance, to the deny things the opportunity to go wrong. Do not do things off of the cuff and set out planning to ad lib. Present only from work and rehearsal you have done thoroughly before facing the prospect.

If your customer says something that is a surprise, you may not have done enough homework or gathered enough intelligence. What do you do if something unexpected comes up? Prepare for the unexpected; adjust, adapt, overcome, and work to deny that opportunity by carefully planning and controlling the call and if all else fails, fall back on a polite "That is a very good question. I will research that further for you, since you deserve good answers, and get back to you within 24 hours."

While a sales manager, my rookie sales woman had been working with same prospect for three months and the deal just didn't seem to be going anywhere. She was doing everything right. The solution was researched, validated, tested, and perfect. Our product was definitely what was needed. But the closing seemed no further along than the first meeting.

I had an idea that maybe trust was the issue. I asked the prospect for a few minutes of his time alone, which he granted. The man was a ring-knocker, proud of his college and football team and his office glaringly reflected his devotion, right down to that huge college ring on his right hand. He was a Southerner from birth. I formulated a plan from what I knew about the man and believed to be the problem.

I explained as the sales manager I could not afford to continue sending the sales woman over to him for meetings that weren't getting either of us anywhere. Didn't he like her? No, he liked her. Was there a question about her competence? No. Did he not see our solution was not only the best but also the most valuable for the price? It is.

"Okay, I think I understand where the issue is. You know there are a couple of things I have learned in this business. Buyers don't trust sales people and I am a sales person. But there is something I will share with you: sales people don't trust buyers and you are a buyer."

A pregnant pause.

"So, now that we have that nonsense on the table, can we brush it off and get down to doing some serious business and get your project off of the dime?"

He leaned back in his chair, took a deep breath and puckered his lips. After about a 10 count, he leaned forward across his desk, as close as he could get to me and said: "You know, you ain't bad at all for a Yankee. Now, what the hell do we have to do to get this darn thing done?"

Strike while the iron is hot.

"Okay, here is what I am going to do. I will send her back to see you this afternoon with the contract for everything we have previously validated and agreed upon. You sign it, but not before she actually asks you for the order, okay? I am trying to develop her and having her believe that she is bringing this in on her own will be good for her and helpful to me."

"Send her over".

John (Doc) Fabiano

I had just got his consent that he was now my partner.

Three hours later he called me to say she was on her way back with his signature on the contract; in his opinion she had done a good job asking for the order. And, he continued to add that since the company was growing rapidly, we needed to meet regularly to keep pace with his needs.

Here is another story from the other side of the coin:

As a regional manager for independent distribution, it was one of my responsibilities to accompany distributor sales people on certain calls, preferably for larger deals. This one telephone company was working a large hospital and the sales manager asked me to accompany one of his more senior reps favorable to my product over the competition.

He was a good guy, but telephone company old school, an order taker and a time waster at best. As we drove to the hospital, I tried to engage him about the meeting plans (of which there didn't seem to be anything concrete) and about the man we were going to meet. They had been friends for some time and been discussing what needed to be done and according to the rep, not much else was required to get the business. The rep just wanted to introduce me as "the factory guy".

It sounded weak, and years on the road had taught me to trust only what I could see and feel.

We walked through the hospital to the contact's office. "Biomed-engineer" read the sign on the door. That the man, in coveralls and a ball cap, had to go to another office to get a folding chair for me to sit on in his closet sized office in the dampest part of the hospital basement should have been reason enough to know that this call was going nowhere.

After about an hour of chit chat of which about 10 minutes was spent on how much he liked our stuff, we shook hands and said good bye. What had been accomplished? Was the process moving along? Not a chance.

A biomed engineer is the Mr. Fixit, a maintenance man in hospital, repairing beds, analog medical devices, and figuring out when to call professional techs from the factory to fix expensive equipment. (By that description, they do not exist anymore.) The only checks he signed were his paychecks so he could deposit them.

The lesson: if you have to ask your supposed decision-making contact to put the broom down to listen to you, chances are, YOU ARE TALKING TO THE WRONG GUY!

Besides meeting with a non-decision maker, that my guy had no plan of any kind didn't move whatever deal he thought he had anywhere. And it was more than just a waste of my time: I had to take three flights to meet with this person in the middle of the middle of something middling.

Qualify and plan, then qualify again. And that includes qualifying your contact for decision making and contract signing abilities.

All that being said, a learned fellow, Lawrence Gitman, has produced ten sales call categories, from worst to best (this guy has been there and has a T shirt to prove it):

1. Worst: the cold call
2. Almost as bad: appointment made from a cold call
3. Semi-good: trade show/networking event
4. Pretty good: social media inquiry
5. Pretty good: web inquiry
6. Pretty good: email blast to existing customers
7. Real good: referral from another customer or friend
8. Real good: unsolicited referral
9. Great: unsolicited call from a prospect wanting to buy
10. Best: unsolicited call from a customer wanting to buy more

CHAPTER 9

You Gotta Love on Your People

I worked for a telecommunications company that had started manufacturing off the shelf, ruggedized, mil-spec computers for the Department of Defense; it eventually went on to manufacturing and selling communication systems. The developers of the company were four "double E's" from a noted university.

Based in California, the company put into effect some new procedures and policies for building and maintaining superb employees. The campus was a few dozen acres of modest, low impact buildings that housed the entire operation, including manufacturing and research and development. The place was lavishly landscaped; it was also water-scaped: ponds, pools, and streams ran throughout the campus creating a most pleasant and serene environment.

It didn't end there. There was a gym with all sorts of equipment and racket sport courts, an Olympic sized pool, athletic and diet/nutrition programs of many different kinds. The cafeteria, open from 6 a.m. to 5 p.m., was one of the best restaurants in the valley and would prepare take home dinners for visitors put up in hotels.

At least once a month, ice cream parties occured and, at the end of each quarter, when good results were reported (they always were good), a Friday afternoon beer blast took place on the greens between buildings;

the limit was three beers each and in those days, considering the loyalty, no one abused the privilege.

Profit sharing was for all, from day thirty of employment, which most of the time meant at least an extra paycheck each quarter. But there was something else that was amazingly outstanding: the "CSL". An employee was entitled to a "continued service leave" after each six years of continuous employment. This was a twelve week leave with full pay and benefits; those on leveraged plans received commissions of an average of the last 36 months. The employee could also take as much vacation time accrued to that time as he or she wanted. And, one could take a six week leave at twice the payment plan, again with vacation days.

For the sales force, they created "President's Club", which was a six-day holiday for all achieving a marked percentage above quota. And all worked very hard and diligently to qualify, as it was one hell of a party held at some four-star resort on the Hawaiian Islands.

Training was exceptional: many levels of product training, sales training, technical training, and management training were carefully planned and delivered. The results of which showed: the company was second to none in the industry, set the bar, and commanded higher prices than the competition.

Employee opinions mattered. Deliberate steps were taken to ensure that not only were the employee comments and suggestions heard, they were encouraged. All, including the contracted night time cleaning crews, felt strong ownership in the company and the results showed.

New hires were given a detailed and leisurely orientation and tour of the campus. Frequently heard was "Wow! We get to work here?" It was hard to believe but did not take much time to acclimate.

Of particular notice and appreciation, was that the four owners had a frequent habit of joining employees at their tables in the cafeteria to chat and listen. None of the management, right up to the owners, wore "badges of rank" and treated all equally.

You could smell, touch, and taste the loyalty and conscientiousness of every single employee. The company was very successful.

The point was well made: to have the best from employees, the company needs to "love on 'em" as well as give them an opportunity for ownership, and train and treat them well.

That led to company employees loving on the customers, which is never a bad thing.

Here are considerations for taking care of your people:

Accepting a "family" style environment is a good and basic starting point. Treat your people, peers, below, and above as you would your own family. Be patient, considerate, empathetic, and prepared to listen as well as endeavor to understand.

As with all good relationships, communication is vital; deliberately and carefully work on improved and non-judgmental communications.

Make "ad hoc" partners with whom you interact regularly.

Make sure each has skin in the game and understands each other's mission and responsibilities, as well as obstacles.

Provide people with the opportunity for "ownership" in strategies, procedures, and plans. Ask for their input.

Make decisions based on validated facts, not hearsay.

Fix problems, not blame.

Understand all sides of the story, the situation, prior to acting.

Take your time to develop a solution; have a solution to the problem rather than lamenting about it.

Allow others authority, keep the responsibility.

Give away the credit, accept the blame.

Act; avoid reacting.

Think before speaking and acting.

Consider consequences, both good and bad. What might be good for the goose, may not be good for the gander.

As humans are gobs of emotion, consider the other guy's feelings as you formulate a response, a solution.

Failure is okay, accept it. We learn from failure and grow from understanding it. Just don't do it twice and work to understand why as to avoid failure again.

TRY EVERY DAY TO MAKE THINGS BETTER FOR THOSE AROUND YOU AND YOURSELF. IT ONLY TAKES A SECOND TO BE NICE AND IT'S FREE.

Now that you understand loving on your people, apply the same to your customers. Everybody needs to feel loved and wanted.

Treat people right and they will reciprocate.

CHAPTER 10

The Basic Sales Process

Somewhere in my rusty and distant past I remember an old chestnut about sales that went "Sales is creating a need and then filling that need". I never could get my arms around that one. Doesn't the customer have some say in the matter?

To be sure there are sales people out there that could sell blubber to Eskimos and sin to Christ but using such skills to sell someone something they did not really need does not strike me as ethical.

Folks want ownership and helping a customer come to his/her own conclusions will carry considerably more weight than any other method, especially a lot more heft than telling the customer what his/her conclusions should be. That does not happen quickly or without subtle encouragement from you.

Think of the sales process as having an "arc".

An "arc" you say? What is that?

All good stories, movies, TV shows, have an "arc", which is to say a beginning, a middle, and an end. An introduction, character introduction and development, plot development, elaboration and sub plots, crisis/conflict/problem, solutions, resolutions, and, conclusion. See if you can apply this to your favorite television show and you will come to understand it. Notice how the steps are ended by commercial breaks, much like intermissions between acts at a play.

In the Middle Ages, an entertainment called "The Morality Play", performed for the masses in town squares and cathedrals, would have an "arc". The play was to show the battle between good and evil and how good always triumphed over evil providing hope for the common man in rather dismal times.

Characters would represent certain virtues and go through development and conflict (and conflict is the essence of drama). The characters would be introduced at the beginning of the "arc" in order that the virtues they represented would become obvious.

Next, complexities and temptations of earthly life would be exposed to create conflict which would continue to increase to the top of the "arc" at which point it would appear that evil would triumph.

The downside of the "arc" would serve to create increased audience interest and excitement as good fought evil until the "Deus ex machina" would provide a glorious resolution.

Now, we are not making a comparison of sales to a battle between the forces of Satan and God, but we are making a comparison of a good sales person and how each "Morality Play" was resolved to the satisfaction of the religious, God-fearing audience: the "Deus ex machina", "The machine of God".

From a platform above the crowd, down would be lowered an "angel", or a "warrior", or a "knight", or an "avenging creature", sent by God, to strike down evil and allow good to prevail. It was the conclusion, the finishing point of the arc. Today we would find such a convention cheesy, but then it was met with cheers and applause since, as was promised, good triumphed.

A good sales person and the prospect go through step by step development, building to the top of an "arc" until an agreement of needs and solutions is reached. The sales person then becomes the "Deus ex machina", bringing to the prospect the solution to problems, cure for ills, a necessary path to satisfying the identified needs, and, in the process, making the prospect a hero for choosing the sales person's solution.

Obviously, there are several steps or "acts" of the sales "arc" that must come first, not to provide conflict and drama, but to exact veracity, validation, and trust.

Allow your point of contact ownership of the process with you and, make sure this individual receives a good measure of recognition for his/her efforts and work. This is simple altruism and you now have a partner rather than a questionably interested or adversarial party.

There are distinct steps between the beginning and the end that must be considered in the sale of any product or service. Remember, however, that less is more and, KISS (Keep it simple....)

Whether one is selling egg beaters or commercial jet aircraft, the process is generic; while each step may have nuances different from other products, certain steps of the process cannot be ignored. It follows, then, that understanding the steps of the process is consistent with what should be an exhaustive emphasis of dotting "I's" and crossing "T's" in order to make sure that nothing is missed and there are no surprises.

Pending the product or service, or situation and specific process, steps may be combined or transparent, but in literal definition, they all exist. Think about it. It is an "arc".

1. Prospect—find opportunities
2. Qualify—determine if the opportunity, the contact is worth the effort
3. Discovery—what the prospect wants, needs, desires
4. Review—make sure you understand the wants, needs, desires
5. Confirm—is your understanding correct

6. Design—what do I have that meets the wants, needs, desires
7. Validate—demonstrate the solution; achieve prospect agreement
8. Propose—Put it in writing; confirm wants, needs, desires, suitable application of solution; it all works the way the prospect wants it
9. Close—ask for the order
10. Follow up—deliver what was proposed and agreed upon; ask for referrals.

PROSPECT

Effective prospecting is examined in a following chapter and is critical to maintain a "pipeline" of opportunities. Sales is a numbers process: the more in the pipeline, the greater the chances are for closed business. Prospecting should be a never-ending task and while there must be times for family and smelling the roses, time alone in the world must always have room for prospecting. A good sales person always has eyes and ears open and is prepared to act in real time.

The most desired prospects comes from referrals: where an existing customer or friend recommends calling on a customer or friend of his or hers suggesting that company or person would benefit from the same product or service. Your "script" for this call should acknowledge that the call is sanctioned by the individual providing the referral and that this person believes your product or service would have value and be beneficial.

Cold calling without referrals takes a lot of time to be productive (about 6.25 hours at 8 calls an hour for one appointment, not necessarily one qualified opportunity), which is why the smart work is homework about that company or person on the other end of the line. Again, prepare a generic script consistent with what you have learned.

QUALIFY

But spending time with just anybody and everybody in the hopes that buying is eminent is not prudent and while it provides the appearance of "working" it is not "producing". Qualification is crucial before preceding and not doing so is risking throwing away effort, time, and resources on either a poor opportunity or the wrong person in the company. Many sales people will waste valuable time by attending to an unqualified prospect simply because access exists and they are not sure or comfortable moving to the required step in the process.

Questions need to be answered: can this company benefit from the sales person's product or service (to include if it can be afforded) and, is the person engaged the correct person to make the final decision, an influencer, a recommender, or just an empty suit or uniform? What is the decision-making process for this company and who makes the final decision? (Keep track of who's who as you do this in order to create an organization chart; better yet, ask for one up front to help you understand the workings of the company and the decision process.)

The larger the company, the less the requirement to make all the sales pitches and meetings directly to the president, the CEO; that person relies on those in positions directly below him/her to take on the due diligence and spend their time and resources working with the sales person for understanding, development, and negotiations.

Many times the CFO (Chief Financial Officer) is the final decision maker, but more times than not that position takes the recommendation of the influencers, and needs the approval of the CEO prior to signing contracts and writing checks provided the deal is financially acceptable by the company's criteria.

There are companies in both private and public sectors that require board of directors' approval prior to accepting the sales person's contract. That takes more work and effort and engaging board members directly and early in the process can be beneficial. What is the board's decision process? Is it time sensitive? What is the decision history? How do you get in front of the board or any individual members?

Understanding the decision process is a priority. For some companies, it is meeting the established criteria for making what is called "the short list"; those items that have already been given space in the annual budget. Within this is coming to know how the financial aspects are established and considered: depreciation, double declining balance, lease vs. ownership, loans vs. cash, and a variety of other methods companies may employ to achieve the best value for the use of their money and the best tax advantages. Knowing this will allow you to prepare an effective and relative financial analysis.

Know this: any company worth its salt will not make a decision unless it can validate how it will provide value, increase profits and production, reduce operating expense, and lead to more business.

Of course, not all are Fortune 500 or similar type companies and there are those where the owner is the main point of contact, makes the final decision, and signs the check. Clearly a simpler process and less time consuming.

Qualifying is part of the process that requires professionalism and delicacy. Ask questions, listen more than talk. Write things down. Still don't understand? Ask again.

Qualifying should also be constant. An experienced sales person qualifies after every step since time lost is time wasted and visa-versa.

In capital sales, the process could take months, sometimes years, and with that amount of potential time investment, it was deadly critical that efforts were leading to a closed deal. Qualifying after every meeting, after each step was demanded; it was done as simply as "We are on the right track, don't you agree?" "Yes" meant keep going but a "No" would get red flags flying. Imagine not doing that and expending months and months to find out the deal wasn't there or went to the competition months before.

Never hesitate to dig deeper to get a clear picture of the prospect's financial situation and condition. It is also helpful to learn of and understand previous decisions as well as the habits and character of the decision makers and influencers.

Further, what products and services are the company using now? If such are predominately those of the competition, then a careful review and reconsideration is most needed. Swimming against the current is not always the most prudent course of action.

How do you collect all of this information? Question. Ask. What is the worst answer? No? At least you will learn if your time has been well spent.

DISCOVERY

Once the qualification requirements are satisfied, the next step is to find out what it is the prospective client needs, wants, desires, and why.

Ask questions, open ended questions; listen. Probe directly but with simplicity and ease. Do not cross examine.

Encourage, allow the prospect to talk and talk and talk. What is the need in its simplest terms? How does the prospect do what he does and why is it done that way? There may be many reasons for the need or there may be just as many for no need. The reasons may be simply personal or highly financially or operationally necessary.

But throughout, be an active listener; besides taking notes, acknowledge the prospect's statements verbally. With larger companies a full-blown survey and a needs analysis may be required; the employees must be interviewed to understand their needs and requirements.

Such may require speaking to and questioning each appropriate employee as to what he or she does, how it is done, what are the obstacles, what works, what doesn't, what, in the employee's view, would make things more effective, less expensive, more profitable, simpler, better, easier. We are all eager to voice our opinions about anything; asking the employees for their thoughts, while possibly time consuming, can be a valuable harvest of information.

The survey step is where needs are discovered and should be exhaustive to the extent and degree of the opportunity. The more the sales person knows about the needs, the more effective he/she is which will lead to better approval by the prospect. The survey is the "smoking gun", the data, the evidence, that will determine if the sales person's application/ solution is not only right, but desirable.

The sanctioned survey (management circulates a memo regarding the purpose of the survey and that cooperation is expected) also is a tremendous learning experience from the standpoint of qualification via the rank and file and for building consensus.

Working with a large mortgage servicing company, the results of our survey pointed to a definite need for our products. The increase in efficiency would be hard to ignore. But the upper management dismissed it as not valid. We asked, and were given permission, to conduct the survey again, just to make sure. When we did, something most valuable happened. Coming around a second time with the same survey told the employees that upper management did not trust them and consequently they came back with more and stronger reasons why the company needed our product. Now the survey results showed dismissal was impossible without causing a full-fledged employee riot.

Done deal.

REVIEW

Following the survey, the information should be organized into a clear, precise, image of the present situation and, clearly, the need for improvement and/or change. And presented to the prospect for acknowledgement, agreement, and, confirmation. Prior to delivering this data, it is sensible to learn how, in the company's expectations, such should be organized and presented, as well as to whom. Consider personalities.

In one such situation our survey indicated that our applications should have been applied much sooner to a large department and a work/time analysis showed a lot of money was wasted and opportunities missed. Presenting that to all involved in the decision process would have been dropping an end of career bomb on the department manager and create quite a dust up of denials at the presentation.

With great caution and delicate professionalism, a meeting was arranged with the head of the company, in private, in his office, after hours. Here no stones were thrown, no judgments' made, no personality conflicts exercised; the data spoke for itself.

We were complimented for the way we handled such a sensitive issue and, as a surprise bonus, we were told that upper management suspected as much and needed a validated reason to make changes, including that manager.

Qualification and close, in advance of schedule, just by doing the right thing, in a good way and at the right time

CONFIRM

At this point, if problems or concerns such as above do not exist, a good sales person will put the results and confirmation in writing and ask the prospect to acknowledge the work with a signature.

Not only is this a "trial close" but it is the "confirmation" step; something that may be used at a later date as required. If sufficient confidence and trust exists, then a signature would not be required. But understanding how and in what order the data should be presented is a smart, professional move.

Ask the prospect how and in what order would be the best for presenting the findings.

While working at corporate headquarters as a marketing manager for a new product about to shift from alpha testing to several beta sites, I was asked to provide an update to market timing and opportunity presentation at what was called the TMT meeting, aka: Top Management Team. Chaired by then CEO, surrounded by the other "C" levels and executive vice presidents, these meetings had a scary reputation and herein, I learned a lot about executive presentations. Don't waste their time. Present the facts in a sufficient but spare format and head off objections and surprises by denying the opportunity for such with planning and hard work.

The product development wasn't going well, something the developers were trying to keep hidden; it wasn't delivering to specifications, and manufacture was suffering several line problems, severely limiting production. Simply put, the developers had under-estimated time needed to get a good product to market.

Knowing that the CEO was a man of little patience who did not suffer fools and that a friend had described presenting at a TMT meeting as "being hung on a meat hook and blown in circles by the breeze" I wanted my presentation to be deliberate and exact. Without thinking about who I was going to talk to, I called the CEO's office. To my surprise, he answered the phone, which told me something about him.

I explained I was on the agenda and I didn't want to waste his time, so would he give me an idea as to what he needed to know. He was actually generous with his time and as I reviewed the outline with him, he would comment, "okay, that's good; no don't need that; give me a little more on this"; and so on. At the end of the call he thanked me for calling and told me he wished more of the presenters would do what I did.

The day of the meeting, I was scheduled in the middle of the agenda. When my turn came, I delivered my presentation with great confidence since I had learned straight from the CEO's mouth what he wanted to hear and what questions he wanted answered. When I asked for questions at the end, the CEO spoke first saying that he had gotten all the information he needed and he didn't have any questions.

Which of course, was a warning to all in the room not to ask any questions. After the meeting, which unfortunately did not go well for most of the presenters, as the CEO passed me leaving the room, he clapped me on the back and grunted "Thank you."

Rare praise from that bird.

<u>DESIGN</u>

Depending on the complexity of the product or service, design will be based on the data secured regarding the need, the application, in order to provide the right, effective, reasonable, sensible, solution. In some cases, this part of the process belongs to the engineer, the sales engineer, "technical" people who aren't paid to sell but to make sure the product does what it was designed to do and meets and exceeds the prospects expectations.

It is important here that the sales person has a good relationship with this group and by providing them with proper, good, and detailed information that should be understood. If the sales person has missed something, that will out and require a do over.

Do not presume to tell the "engineer" what to do, his job, as intruding into another's area of expertise does not a good and productive relationship make.

Here the sales person needs to provide all the information and data he/she has uncovered; if this is a complex product, then the engineers should be in attendance at the discovery/survey. It is also a good idea, to include a briefing on the company and personalities.

If this is not a complicated product, then he or she is the one who needs to prepare the solution with the product at hand. Here he or she has to know what's what.

VALIDATE

Validation is the test: does it do what we want and need it to do? Generally, if this step is needed, it isn't a bad idea to do it first without the prospect present, which should be self-explanatory. Once satisfied there will be no surprises, conduct the validation, or demonstration, with the correct members of the organization: the influencers and decision makers.

Taking them to another good customer site using similar applications is a smart idea. But make sure it is a good and happy customer first. Sometimes a small gift of thanks, such as flowers for the front office, may be appropriate to present to the host customer after the fact.
Take care of your friends and keep your customers happy.

Be good and kind to those you engage during your career; you will never know when you may need them again.

Validations also include financial analysis, time benefits analysis, cost of ownership comparisons, and the like.

Regardless of what some folks say about "figures lying and liars figuring", hard data is difficult to ignore. In any of the analysis or study summaries always use the prospect's numbers and formulas to avoid validity questions. Can the prospect argue with his/her own numbers? Vette these exercises deliberately and in detail; deny surprises the opportunity to pop up by being exact and covering all the bases.

PROPOSE

The proposal now should be a fait accompli, a foregone conclusion if you have secured the format your prospect expects and wants to see.

Within a good proposal is the executive summary: a precise, one-page statement summarizing the need, the solution, and the benefits.

Next should be an explanation of the need, the solution, and the benefit in some detail. Validation is provided by a financial analysis that may include cost of ownership over a period of time, anticipated increased production, profitability, decreased operating expenses. The important thing is to clearly show that the solution has merit and benefits connected to dollars and "sense" and, in some cases, a work study analysis tied to salaries is valuable. Keep it simple and concise.

Most companies will have a time tested and proven proposal outline.

Include references, a log of what tasks were accomplished to provide the correct solution, an installation timeline/schedule, and a specific thank you to those employees who participated in the process.

Always include leasing papers, loan applications, other necessary documents, and definitely, the contract.

It is vital that your prospect inspects the proposal in detail and you should take him/her through it—your way. You put a lot of work into this and you don't want anything to be missed that could lead to surprises or misunderstandings later.

You must get the proposal into the right hands: decision makers.

I had to good fortune to work with a high performing rep who understood how to make things his, especially the proposal reading. My friend (we will call him "Karuffie") had a mildly harsh urban accent: "hey, howyadoin, heh?..." He was a good man through and through and a fine husband and father, but, nature had not been kind to him: within hours of a close shave, he had a full day's growth of beard. Although he bought good quality, well-tailored suits, he always looked as if he had slept in them. He didn't have hair on his head, he had small gauge stiff wires upon which a couple of gallons of hair gel would have been wasted.

Despite all that, his prospects and customers loved him, because, simply, Karuffie was Karuffie and his sincerity was impossible to dismiss.

When it came to review the proposal, Karuffie would actually get on his knees on the prospect's side of the desk and deliberately go through his proposal, not just page by page, but sentence by sentence and frequently ask: "So you see why that's so important?" And not continue until he got a verbal acknowledgement.

Karuffie had one of the most extra-ordinarily high closing ratios in our group at the time and rookies would frequently beg to accompany him on proposal deliveries.

<u>CLOSE</u>

Once the potential customer and the sales person have reviewed the contract and all questions answered, on both sides, the sales person closes. Which is to say, he/she asks for the order, the contract, the business, the deal. The sales person should have been doing this with each step, always asking in one way or another if the prospect is ready to go, to sign, to accept the terms of the contract.

However there are, and will continue to be, more than enough literature and conversations about the complexities and vagaries of closing that have a tendency to make the rookie or insecure sales person frightened of this step. It has been overdone and what is a simple step has been over complicated many times over. Keep it simple...

Understand there are volumes and volumes on a multitude of closing techniques; everybody has a method that works, some more complicated than others. Try those that make sense to you, but only after you have made them yours.

Let's make this clear: closing is simple: all one has to do is ask.

Being rather jovial about life, I found I could get away with a lot others couldn't by just being me. I had learned early on that folks will remember things more if I could make them smile, even more so if I could make them laugh (but without being a buffoon). And, since I wanted the prospect to enjoy the experience as much as possible I kept things upbeat. So, at times when a potential impasse loomed I would simply say after that awkward silence, "So, we got a deal?" Or "How do like me so far?" I may not have gotten the deal at that moment, but the response to the good humor and joie de vie would tell me a lot and often unearth objections that had yet to be discovered.

Laughter is the best medicine.

If the proposal is a fait accompli, then delivery and presentation of it is assumed as a yes and a commitment.

FOLLOW-UP

Follow up by keeping regular contact with the customer. Make sure all things contracted for and/or promised are attended to. Always do what you said you will do or were asked to do as well as on time. Keep the customer informed of latest developments and trends. Always ask if the customer will be a reference and, above all, ask for referrals.

Consider establishing a "track" with your prospect at the very start of the process. This is a simple document that connects each step of the process, all that needs be done to reach acceptable solutions and contracts to a calendar. At an early meeting with your qualified point of contact ask what he/she needs done; explain then what you have to do to secure the correct and proper data and information to those needs as well as do your job correctly and completely.

Break down each step as to who does what, when, how long it will take, and always include time for review and confirmation. Here you have tied your prospect into becoming your partner, as you cannot do all this alone without his/her assistance and your track, for which you have secured acceptance, will indicate who does what (you and the prospect) and when. A good track will include the close, the contract signing several steps before completion, allowing for delivery and installation necessities.

See "Appendix 3" for a sample track.

CHAPTER 11

Objections; Questions

If you give it some thought, you may come to realize that an objection is really a question and if you are on the ball and know your stuff as well as your prospect, you should already have a solid answer.

Listen carefully, repeat the question, ask the prospect for confirmation that you fully understand the objection/question, and politely and slowly provide your answer; then ask why the question is being asked and, if are there any others. Conclude this exchange by saying that the prospect should never hesitate to ask a question or express a concern.

Never call an objection an "objection" as that has a rather negative connotation; it is a question that indicates your prospect needs to understand something either he doesn't or is expressing a concern about what he knows or has heard that is not in line with the needs, wants, or solution he is seeking. Or, it is an indication of something not liked or accepted favorably. It may even be a signal that your prospect doesn't like or trust you.

It is incumbent on you to discover what motivated this question, and, in some cases, why it comes up now, rather than sooner. You should understand where, when, and how to employ open and closed question skills. Here, as a professional serious about your relationship with the prospect, you need to be cautious, delicate, and certainly not condescending.

I write condescending as I have seen numerous sales people, either possessing too large an ego or worn down by objections, and questions, come back, shall we say, "heavy", in tone and response, clearly indicating in a non-verbal way that the customer doesn't know what he is talking about, is questioning integrity, or has pushed the sales person to the end of patience. Such will absolutely create an adversarial atmosphere and there in, the deal dies.

How would you react to such a response?

Delicate, deliberate, professional, knowledgeable, polite, and concerned...consider these as you answer. I cannot emphasize this enough.

You must also consider an objection/question as an opportunity for further qualification and closing. Some would tell you to answer; "Well, if I can satisfy that question, do we have a deal?" While a "quid pro quo" may seem like a reasonable business response, it creates an imbalance in the harmony of the relationship, which a smart prospect will see as a weakness or indication of insecurity and endeavor to leverage the sales person for more than the original goal. A "quid pro quo" often times is seen as the correct response, but I find it rather pedestrian.

As the right word may be worth a thousand pictures, use your skills and knowledge of the prospect to build an elegant "trial close" along the same lines, but nowhere near as blatant and crude as the "quid pro quo".

Nobody likes to be called "simple" or "stupid" much less having the question that is important to him or her blown off as trivial and not important.

Every question and statement your prospect makes IS important and it is your responsibility to make sure he feels that it is. This is the real "quid pro quo", a tacit one: if you want him or her to recognize you as important, you must extend the same courtesy to him or her. No matter how unreasonable or unknowledgeable your prospect may be, you need to make him or her feel smart, aware, and on the same level with you. But you must be sincere; consider that most prospects have a superior sense of "smell" allowing them to detect fear or anything that is not supported by confidence or untrue.

The best way to overcome the objection/question(s) is to deny them the opportunity to come up.

Now, what the heck is that? How do you deny an objection/question? Tell the prospect you reject it flat out and either won't or don't need to respond?

No. You work smart and plan in advance; and keep notes or an outline of responses to objections you suspect may exist.

You must know your stuff and from experience and comparing notes with your peers, detail at where and what objections and questions historically arise. You should write down the objections/questions that you haven't heard before so, at you leisure, you can formulate a sound and respectful responses as preparation for a later engagement.

As you now have sound understanding of the standard objections/ questions, work the answers into your dialog, so the answer is evident before the question is asked. You have denied the objection/question before it came up.

Simple, right? Well, not at first, because this takes experience and knowing how to work smart, both of which you may accelerate by being a good listener, comparing notes with your peers, and having no fear to ask your own group questions on matters that are of concern to you.

Do not expect this approach to work as smooth as silk the first time you attempt it, but to do it right, you need to plan before your meeting, your dialog, and seek out every part of the anticipated conversation or presentation that either you know could bring up an objection/question or suspect could do the same. If you have done your job correctly you will know your prospect and his or her "hot and cold buttons" which could appear if you stray into uncharted waters where you do not know how the prospect will react. If you know your prospect, you can avoid stumbling into quicksand by not doing a dump of everything you know, regardless of the connection to the solution, (while seeking to improve your esteem with the prospect), and inadvertently bring anything up that is not going to sit well and create a problem or hurdle for you to overcome; you do not need to make any problems for yourself.

They will appear on their own.

As an example: do not rattle on about your qualms and peeves about your wife to your mother-in-law. Bad, bad, bad.

Get the picture?

Be deliberate in your planning, and when you think you have overturned every stone, work back to front seeking more stones to upend.

Objections/questions are flags of opportunity and if you listen carefully and remember what you have heard you may assemble the pieces of a puzzle that will elegantly bring you and your prospect to a condition of mutual acceptance and agreement (i.e.: close).

CHAPTER 12

Profitable Prospecting

So, you got the job, a new suit, polished shoes, a lap top, maybe even a briefcase, and, of course, a phone.

A phone. You are about to discover that handset can weight over 300 pounds if you cannot make this basic device your friend. And, if it feels that heavy the first time you pick it up, chances are you are in the wrong job.

Which is okay; the first step to salvation is to admit you want salvation or, at least, another, if not, better, job.

Where do your customers come from?

They come from prospects.

So, where do prospects come from?

Well, first off, you need to determine how many prospects you need to secure one contract, one deal. National averages point to 25% closing ratios, meaning that of four prospects, you may close one.

If you can get your arms around that, it is a good start.

But, the phone isn't really your friend on day one, unless you start advertising to your "warm market", aka: your family, friends, neighbors, business acquaintances, church members, volunteer partners, in-laws, and whomever else you can think of. You should take the time to make a list of anyone you know that would give you enough time to tell your news about your new job and product or service in (in this case) about 100 well chosen, interesting words or slightly more. Then, listen to the response and then ask if they would like to hear more; even if yes or no, ask for a referral to another person or people.

Think big—and—think socially here and start connecting and building up a list of warmer prospects based on your "friends and family leverage". These are people you may approach with the recommendation and sanction of someone they know but you don't and now would have reason to extend to you the courtesy of a phone call, a meeting.

Join local organizations, if you haven't already: Rotary, local business clubs and organizations, as well as pay for membership networking organizations or the premium networking websites. This is basic networking and if you cannot network, you will have a very short sales career life span.

Starting out, you have to do this. The more time you put in now, the better shape you will be in later. You will also learn a lot. Here, as with all things, set goals: so many hours a day, so many real-time contacts, etc. Don't stop until you have more than quadrupled your contacts several times over.

An acquaintance of mine got a job selling new cars. In that business, sales people work alternate shifts: some days 8 to 5, some 11 to close, always Saturdays, all day, and sometimes, Sundays. My friend worked what is known in the car business as "bell to bell"—open to close every day, every weekend, and as a result harvested more prospects than the other sales reps, which, as he got better at his selling skills, led him to the top of the heap and to the sales manager position in less than a year.

And then he began to give himself some time off, shortly after he purchased a nice fat house for himself and his family.

What you don't want to do is sit at a desk looking at a phone and making calls from a cold list (names of people to whom there is no immediate or recognized connection). At an average of 8 calls per hour, it takes the average sales person 6.25 hours to make one appointment. If your closing ration is 25%, or one out of four, that means you are on the telephone 25 hours to have one possible, not guaranteed prospect.

Doesn't make much sense, does it?

Here are a couple of other bits of data: nationally, only 2% of cold calls result in an appointment and, inside recommendations (not cold calls) account for about an 82% success rate, while only 20% come from what are considered to be "effective" cold calls. Not every appointment results in a qualified opportunity or a possible proposal; the ratios here are low in terms of proposals from cold calling appointments. They are better from referral appointments.

See how that phone can be heavier than a dumb bell? (Pun intended).

If you stop and think, there are prospects all around you. You should know by now the strengths and weakness of your product and what it can and cannot do for customers. What is the target market? Keep your eyes open; ransack business lists, journals, the local paper. Zero in on those businesses that you believe may have a need, then start with the intelligence you have gathered.

Anybody in the office or any of your social acquaintances know anything about that company? Check the local newspaper/media archives; check Angie's List, Yelp, the BBB; Google the company; Google the company for customer reviews; Google the company for employee reviews (this often tells you a great deal).

Act, do not react. Build a dossier on this company. What do they do? Do they do it well? How long have they been in town? How many people do they employ? What is their market and how wide and deep is it? What is the annual pre-tax production in dollars? What is the financial credit rating? What separates this company from others of its kind? Is it growing, expanding, or reducing? Who is who—what does the organization chart look like? And probably another couple of dozen questions you can think of on your own.

Now you know enough to determine if and with whom a meeting is worthwhile. Your research has given you enough to tailor and refine your "introduction" to specific resonance rather than a generic collection of words.

Stimulate interest.

Stimulate conversation.

Plan smart; work smart.

Ask open ended questions. (These are questions that require more than a yes or no answer; questions that start providing details).

Take notes. (1) Try as you might, you cannot remember everything. (2) People respond well when they recognize that you are actually listening to them and taking notes is a simple way to demonstrate that you are, in fact, listening.

Ask for an introductory meeting with the appropriate employees/ upper management using a closed ended question that offers a choice of a couple of days: Which day? Yes or no? Think of it as a "closing", something you should be doing frequently.

In the telecommunications industry we had a saying: "The good news is, every company needs a telephone system. The bad news is every company needs only one." If we had kept with that line of thinking, then we would have only secured appointments with new companies, which would have sorely limited opportunities. But, we knew our stuff and the competitions' stuff and knew that the average life span of a telephone system back then was about five years before growth or obsolescence demanded a replacement. Now we had a lot more opportunities and discovering how "old" that building was became important as did understanding technological trends and relationships to different industries.

Something else to consider.

Remember, be "in" the world, not "of" the world; use that same thinking when it comes to the business community in which you operate. Make no mistake, it is not all ice cream and cake out there ("We did not come this far by being made of cotton candy." Winston Churchill). No one is going to give you a meeting just because you asked; you must distinguish yourself and your product from the start.

"Stop interrupting what people are interested in and BE what people are interested in." (We said that before, but repeating these words here is appropriate.)

CHAPTER 13

Making It Yours

In the early days of interconnect, I was working for a private distributor of large scale telephone systems manufactured by a company I was soon to join and with whom make my career. The manufacturer had sent a representative to deliver a series of training presentations meant to drastically improve product knowledge (of which we knew very little), application knowledge (of which we knew even less), and techniques employed to sell the product (we were not selling many).

By the time this person was finished with his tasks I had already decided that was what I wanted to do and that his company, was, absolutely, the one I wanted to be a part of

This person, whom we shall call Ray, knocked all of us out of our socks with his presentation skills and personality, his complete command of his subjects, and his infectious enthusiasm. He didn't read the slides (this was way before PowerPoint and the proliferation of laptops) but spoke from them. He barely looked at the screen, but knew each slide as it came into view. He had a great sense of timing, a delightful sense of appropriate humor, and a delivery that was natural, elegant, and so simple it was the cleanest I had ever seen.

Not one "ah", "um", "er", or similar drops in the rhythm. (In acting class the saying was: "There are no "uh's" in Shakespeare.")

Ray knew his stuff and could do it in his sleep, standing atop Everest, fighting a bull in a ring with a red cape, doing barrel rolls in an F-18, or any other situation that might require singular concentration.

He got us fired up, enthused, eager to go forth and prosper.

And all of my peers fell flat on their faces in a week or less.

Why?

Because they all tried to "do" Ray and duplicate his style. But nobody but Ray could do "Ray".

Ray was so good because, among other things that manifested focused work and effort, he knew who he was and what worked and did not work for him alone.

Which is a round-about allegory to get to the point of this chapter: make it yours. Whatever it is that requires delivery by you, make it yours.

Mel Gibson's portrayal of Hamlet was different that Richard Burton's, whose delivery was different that of Sir Laurence Olivier, yet all were equally compelling with their time in front of the camera or on the stage.

They all knew the script, the play, verbatim.

How did they do that?

Well, any good artist will tell you that 90% of creativity is theft that then is made highly personal and was one of the first things I learned in art and theatre school.

With the Hamlet example, each actor took what was already there, already proven, on the page and made it theirs. Gibson brought a modern vitality and amusing craziness to the role; Burton made Hamlet vibrate with that sonorous and glorious Welsh voice; and Olivier walked the boards playing himself, above it all, deliberately announcing he was king of all the actors in the world. All three brought the prince of Denmark to life and true to Shakespeare's words.

When I hear of sales people talking about having to learn a script, a pitch, a presentation, verbatim, I cringe; kind of like the sound of fingernails scraping down a chalk board. The idea of a concise sales script is sound, because it has all playing the same sheet of music, but not everyone is the same instrument.

We are all different, beyond the fact that our ability to cook our food and accessorize our garments separates from the animals.

What I would rather hear is: "Here is the scripted message; now, make it work by making it yours."

Customers respond to the visual and the tone of the sound. They will also remember more of what is delivered if it made them smile, confirmed their interest, provided a laugh, and kept them awake.

When you are handed the "memorize verbatim" assignment you may want to think of how you said your prayers as a kid: the words were always the same, but there was no recognition, no emphasis, no meaning, no soul. You rattled them off just to get it done and resume what you had been doing before with a minimum of interruptions.

Here is a little saying to keep in mind as you work with scripts, pitches, and presentations: "You will never mean what you say unless you can say what you mean." And you can't do that by being somebody you are not.

So, how do you go about "making it yours"?

It is going to take work, preferably in private, and (this may come as a surprise) in front of a mirror. The best actors I knew and worked with during my first career in theatre talked about "bedroom work" as how they prepared the characters they were to play. They would lock themselves in their bedroom and practice their lines in front of a mirror over and over again until they had the words cold, and were satisfied that their delivery, expression, and movement fit the character as they wanted it seen for that moment in time as scripted. Alone in their bedrooms, they could try different speech patterns, deliveries, expressions, until what they believed worked so simply for them, it existed as part of them.

A fine actor on the stage never looks like he is struggling with his work.

Practice over and over. Practice until it sounds comfortable to you. Practice until it sounds like you. It should not be stilted or dissonant. You should not only like what you see in the mirror, but actually enjoy what you see.

Think elegant, smooth, seamless, and simple. You may wish to change a word here or there or re-arrange the order, but always keep to the message, provided that the message as scripted is clear to you. (Because if it isn't, how can you make it clear to your audience?) Keep at it; it may take more than several rehearsals to get it to where you are very satisfied with the results.

You may speak a message with your words, your way and I may speak the same message with my different words but we can still deliver the intended result by delivering it, with confidence, as uniquely ours.

So, don't try to "do" Ray. Steal what he does that appeals to you, make it yours, and bring that to the message. Make it yours.

Get to the point, validate the point, and make it resonate to the situation and audience. Mike Schultz's blog talks to sales in terms of resonance, differentiation, and substantiation.

Keep it simple, straight forward, and fluid. Above all, make it yours.

CHAPTER 14

Presentations

Did you know that there are some performers out there who get so frozen from stage fright they literally have to be pushed on to the stage? I would mention a few here that are still alive, but I don't want to get sued. A former popular "beach movie" starlet, after her movie career ended, took to dinner theatre work and literally had to be thrown out on to the stage to make her first entrance. Once on the boards, however, she was a consummate professional.

So, if thinking about speaking in public makes you freeze up, you are not alone and, in pretty good company.

A presenter needs energy to make his/her work come alive and be animated. If that energy isn't there and properly channeled, the act will be as exciting as watching paint dry. Stage fright can be channeled into energy and most good actors rely on it to make their performances bright and new.

Most people are not comfortable speaking in public and making presentations simply because they haven't done much of it; and even more likely, they haven't been shown how to do it.

So, let's talk first about delivery, your physical presence. You must be comfortable with what you are wearing; remember that old saying "Don't compete with your clothes". It may sound silly, but if something about what you are wearing is on your mind, it will affect your performance. (And yes, think performance). As well, don't wear anything that could be even mildly construed as disturbing or uncomfortable to the audience. Look professional, shoes shined, suit and shirt pressed, no ties with topless hula dancers, well groomed, nothing that could be distracting to your audience.

If you are experiencing any nervousness, don't be alarmed. That is normal for most people. A good way to deal with that is an isometric of pushing your hands together with strength; it is an old actor's trick. Focus on your breathing; count the duration of your inhales and exhales so you can comfort yourself that you are not breathing rapidly and heavily. Close your eyes and attempt to clear your mind of anything but the task at hand. That will be difficult, because the mind is like a monkey: rapidly moving all over the place. You will probably agree. However, with focus and concentration you can gain some control and visualize the task at hand.

You have probably heard of "mindfulness"; it is a hot word and concept these days. What it really means, going back to early Tibetan teachings, is to be in the "moment", the "now".

It is a state of being clearly aware of all parts and senses of your immediate environment and not losing concentration on the past or the future. Your focus is intensified and clearer the more you learn how to be "mindful".

Mind your posture. Stand straight up; plant your feet firmly on the floor, as if you are attached to it, grounded. Smile. Not some goofy, "I am as nervous as hell" grin, but a confident expression, kind of like the cat that ate the canary.

Scan your audience before you open your mouth. This is you acknowledging their presence which is a good, non-verbal message to send out. This will also allow you to pick out accepting and non-accepting faces in the crowd, also something important to know. There is usually someone in the front row grinning ear to ear as well as some grumpy frowner. You will have to play to each, so you might as well know where they are from the start.

Speak calmly, with authority, and loud enough to be heard by all. You need to project your voice by speaking from your diaphragm, not your throat and mouth. Your diaphragm is just below your breast plate, around your belly button. Place your hand there and feel it expand and contract as you breathe normally. Now with your hand there, standing erect, shoulders straight, legs straight, feel the expansion and contraction as you speak in harmony with your breathing. Singers need to breathe rapidly or slowly depending on lyric and tempo, exercising trained breath control; but you are speaking, not singing, so a constant breath pattern of drawing in and exhaling is not only important but critical. Ever choke up speaking when you are excited? You don't want that.

Speaking from your diaphragm, try to bounce your voice off of the back wall of the room. Enunciate. Speak normally, not rapidly and not slowly. Always ask if all can hear you clearly. "Clearly" is important as you may be heard, but not understood.

By rehearsing the presentation and with your knowledge of the audience, place emphasis with your voice on those points and words that demand it. You may also use the "pregnant pause" to allow the meaning to sink in. Just stop talking and count to five before speaking again.

Don't drone, that is, fall into a repeating pattern or rhythm of speech which will turn off your audiences' listening capacity and lead to "fanny fatigue" (people beginning to fidget in their seats), yawns, coughs, and head nodding. Be aware of these signals from your audience and change tempo, volume, and position to keep their attention.

Which gets us to movement. Don't stand in one place; it's boring. Personally, I never liked making a presentation from a podium and I never made a presentation sitting down. You should consider doing the same. Sitting down tells your audience you are not that interested in them and that is a turn off. But, then again, don't jump around, either. Consider your surroundings and the shape of the space you are working in. The center always gives you the most focus, but moving slowly to five or six points from the center, while sounding silly, is, in fact, more interesting. Avoid showing your back to the audience and stay in the light.

Depending on the situation and circumstances, you may request the audience hold their questions to the end or to the end of the "session" if the presentation is broken into parts divided by "intermissions" for relief, coffee, snacks, or meals. Generally, this is a good idea as you want to maintain your rhythm and momentum as well as keep on schedule. Time is important as the average homo sapien's attention span begins to flag after about 40-45 minutes. Unfortunately, the younger the audience, the shorter the attention span.

However, if you are presenting to the board of directors, "C" levels, the apex decision makers, take questions as they come up; write them down for future reference. Lacking an immediate answer, respond by announcing a time and date when you will return with the answer.

Stand-up comedians have a variety of methods to shut down hecklers, who are occupational hazards for them. In a professional, business format, those methods are not appropriate and would cost you all the good will and trust you have built up.

But what do you do with an audience member that keeps speaking to another person loud enough for all to hear? You stop talking and focus your attention to that person. Be calm and patient, and your audience will do the work for you, by staring at the offender.

If you are faced with a relentless questioner, trying either to trip you up or demonstrate how much he/she knows, tell him/her that you will take his questions at the end of the presentation, in order that you may continue for the rest of the audience.

If you have done your job well, you will have won over the majority of the audience and by focusing your silence on the "hecklers" the audience will do the work for you.

You have probably heard this before: "Never let them see you sweat."

These days, the average person visits the cell phone more times in waking hours than we might believe possible. You certainly do not want to present to an audience who's every face is staring into a tiny, hand held screen.

Politely ask that all cell phones be turned off, as not to disturb others in the audience. To turn off the phone is a courtesy and to spend time staring into the phone during someone's presentation is just downright rude. It is up to you to find ways that work for you to avoid this epidemic problem.

The preparation itself with all the software and applications available can be very simple, or very complicated. Just remember: "KISS", keep it simple, stupid. Leave the heavy duty, slickly produced, high graphics, and animations to the television commercials. Don't try to do all or any sorts of fancy stuff; 1) It really doesn't impress your audience and 2) You most likely are not a professional who can produce high quality work.

Keep it tight and concise and resonant to the audience. Less is more.

While studies have shown visuals are processed some 60,000 times faster than text, which supports the saying "A picture is worth 1000 words" consider also that sometimes the right word is worth a 1000 pictures. Consider the vernacular of your audience and prepare appropriately.

Start out with an outline of what you want to communicate. Main ideas, elaboration, validation, solution, benefit, value. Good rules to follow: have a concise agenda slide to start following your title slide; put no more than 3 – 5 points on a slide; keep you slide free of graphics clutter; choose a conservative, suitable background and format; if you must use animation, keep it simple, as in producing each point one at a time, just don't over-do it; allow yourself plenty of time to complete the presentation; have a concise summary slide that is followed by a call to action.

You may wish to take your outline and transpose it to the PowerPoint outline, so you may have a reproducible, hard copy of the work. Generally, not a bad idea, as it allows you to put more than one slide on a piece of paper with room for notes.

Organize your presentation as you would with your writing. Tell 'em what you are going to tell 'em; tell 'em; tell 'em you told 'em. Make your points from the most important on down. Keep it simple, clear, and concise and, always on the issue.

Here is what really separates the pros from the amateurs: never read the slide, talk from it. You embellish each point, you build your case around each point. The presentation should obviously give the audience credit for having brains; your embellishment further establishes that and credits them for their ownership of same. It is best if you don't look at the slide at all.

Such a professional performance can only enthrall and confirm great competence. Just that convention of never looking at the slides will create a great impression and close the books on any questions about your professionalism and confidence in your work.

Part of our visually dominated attention spans points to at least 64% of your audience will remember stories above statistics. Be cautious when working with statistics, tables, and charts; they can be deadly for a variety of reasons. Studies have shown that the average audience is more interested in visuals than statistics, so you need to find a way to wrap the numbers into something engaging; here again you need to know your audience. Tables and charts have a habit of reproducing too small to have impact and might require the use of a pointer or facing the screen to make indications. Better to provide the audience with hard copies of such things so you can make your points clearly and concisely, free of clutter.

To accomplish all of this, you must know your presentation cold and it must absolutely be "yours". Remember "bedroom work" mentioned in the "Make It Yours" chapter? Do the same with your presentation. Rehearse, rehearse, rehearse. Analyze, edit, rewrite, proofread. Leave no stone unturned and don't take the show on the road until you can do it in your sleep. That's what any good performer would do. Consider doing a "dress rehearsal" in your office for your peers first.

Yes, it sounds like a lot, but, if you have made it this far, I'll bet you can do it if you are serious.

Have fun doing it. Folks don't respond very well to watching people work.

CHAPTER 15

The Reality Pill

Robin Williams once said: "Reality, wow! What a concept".

He had it right.

In sales, reality has many, many definitions, all put forth by people who feel strongly about what ever has their attention at the time. At issue is whether or not their reality means anything to anyone else.

Reality comes in many forms, some driven by denial of the truth of the matter at hand, others created to satisfy or please people farther up the food chain, or simply as confirmation that the owner of that particular reality knows more than anybody else.

Or, in the true Buddhist sense, "what is, is."

But, there is only one reality and that is the reality of the moment, that which is around you and your prospect, your customer, as you venture together towards goals that are mutually rewarding. It is a word we mentioned previously: "mindful".

It boils down to simply knowing your stuff, which is to say all that surrounds your efforts to produce by providing solutions, cures, fixes, and applications that satisfy customer needs and therefore result in benefits. You must know your product, its applications, what it does, how it does it, who needs it and why, as well as (gasp) its weaknesses and soft spots. This also implies that you know your competition at least as well as the competition does, if not better. You should also be cognizant of what is happening in your industry and related trends.

However, smart and deliberate use of this knowledge works a whole lot better than spewing out all of what you know every chance you get. The prospect isn't so much concerned about how much you know, but how his/her need will be satisfied, the problem solved and fixed.

Another study reported that buyers value competence over the quality of the offering and the recommended solution up to twice that of price. Competence comes from the clear communication of why and how your product and solution is the best.

As a shallow brook makes the most noise, so should you administer your knowledge sparingly, as needed and without judgment or emotion. Use your wisdom wisely and where and when it does the best for your favor.

Working in a rapidly developing and changing high technology world meant regular introductions of new applications, products, and software. In a high tech industry we were frequently inflicted with product managers shilling their new stuff as the best, better than the competition, and, always, without problems or glitches. They were paid to be advocates for their products, but they also needed to understand the entire picture, which they rarely did.

We were the Independent Distribution Division and at the time, the 72 of us, including inside support and administration, were producing almost 25% of the pre-tax revenue of a billion dollar a year company of almost 10,000 employees.

But the added value we brought to the table was that we worked closely with our distributors, who by nature of being distributors, sold products other than ours, namely our competition. And, because of that, we knew the competition very well indeed. (Okay, I am bragging, but why the hell not?)

John (Doc) Fabiano

While not looking at the market through the myopic eyes of a singular product and set of applications, we got to see what the distributors saw, which was a broad vision encompassing just about everything that was out there. The direct sales force had no such opportunities to see the total market the way it really was.

Many in the company did not know we existed; we were a band of wild outlaws, working with very enlightened management, on our own, making our own decisions, and being strong advocates for our distributors. And since we were not "broken" the upper, upper management didn't try to fix us and left us alone.

The product managers had come to fear presenting to our group since we had proven we knew what was going on better than they and that they were programmed only to appease the upper management. By the nature of their jobs and position within the inside of the company, they acted as if they knew better, but in the end, they didn't know everything. And we were not shy about voicing our opinions and what we knew was fact out in the real world.

This was clearly a reason why our production, per capita, outstripped the larger, direct sales force.

Working as we did with the distributors and learning from them, we daily and happily swallowed the reality pill. There was what was really happening and not what others thought was happening.

A good sales person is not myopic nor looks at the world through rose colored glasses. Going forth with a narrow vision limited to THE product is a formula for failure. Nor does a good sales person hold forth as knowing all that is needed to know but rather is hungry to learn more. He/she sees the world for what it is right now.

Do your homework, due diligence, research. And do not fear suspicion, it keeps you sharp and frequently leads to what is really true.

Beware of the supposed simple assignment or sale. Few things are actually what they appear to be.

Very long ago, fresh out of college, I got a job selling radio advertising at a station in that college town. I was assigned my first opportunity by the sales manager: renew a thick, annual contract with a ski shop. According to the sales manager this was a done deal, a piece of cake, since that store owner had bought a custom jingle that required a twelve month contract the year before and consequently she would want to get the most out of it again this year.

Right.

The owner immediately told me she was not interested in renewing since she did not see much of an increase in business from ads with the custom jingle. In fact, she was not happy (something I learned later that she frequently was), and about ready to sever ties with my station and give her business to the only other station in town.

It took a great deal of effort to get her to sign a reduced contract and a lot of follow up on my part to put a smile back on her face. It was nowhere near what the sales manager said it would be.

A done deal? Not even close.

The sales manager had not done his homework, was oblivious to the facts, and merely assumed all was okie-dokie with the ski shop owner. His reality was really a dream.

Remember: question.

Taking your daily reality pill keeps denial out of your psyche and enables you to recognize when another's denial of the facts, either deliberate or nurtured by fear of failure, can screw up the works if you let it fester.

Reality, wow! What a concept.

CHAPTER 16

The Value Proposition

Remember we said earlier "You will never mean what you say unless you can say what you mean"? Then here is where the rubber meets the road, so to speak.

The value proposition is a simple statement that concisely and clearly communicates what the product does and how it uniquely provides value to the user. It should be worded to be compelling and interesting, yet short and simple enough to not tax immediate recognition.

Some refer to the value proposition as a "concept", which can be argued for. But at its best, it is a simple statement that can be embellished appropriately as needed in order to resonate with each specific prospect. It should be memorized as if a "mantra" and delivered with the ownership of each sales person, which is to say, with individual rhythm and emphasis.

If it doesn't sound right to you, then it certainly isn't going to sound right to the prospect.

But a value proposition isn't what has been slung around as an "elevator" pitch, the idea that one can convey a great deal of information, seemingly on the fly in less than 60 seconds. Folks who try to decimalize the attention span of humans are fond of saying how short that attention span is, but forget that strong, intelligent, engagement accounts for uninterrupted attention.

As an example, your value proposition is: "Our custom coded call center software produces improved performance and shortened holding times resulting in more revenue for each company's unique market and traffic to which our many customers can attest."

Now, you are in an elevator with someone who is in upper management with some large retail website and he has just mentioned that they are stymied by long holding times after many attempts to fix the problem. You pull your value proposition out of your holster and then follow with: "If I could demonstrate how my product solves that problem, as it has with many other call centers, all specific to their individual needs, would you be interested?"

Could he say no to that? Well, maybe, as there are no absolutes, but, the chances are, if you look and sound the part and speak with confidence and authority, he will say, at least, "tell me more."

Do not be lured into a "value proposition" or "elevator pitch" simply based on someone's theory that most people don't have a brain, including you and the prospect. Know your value proposition, yourself, and how to listen; and, (as said before) sometimes the right word is worth 1000 pictures.

Think first, speak second. And always give the other guy credit for having a brain; sooner or later that credit will be validated or discredited by his speech and actions.

As you develop your value proposition first include all that comes to mind that could make sense; don't be concerned about length but more about writing your ideas down as to what might make the point. Then start taking out those pieces that first come to mind as not directly supporting the message.

Write, edit, repeat. (Lather, rinse, repeat—the meaning of life).

Continue to do so until you are satisfied with a few words that make sense delivering the message as defined above and sound right as you speak them. "This is what my product does and this is how it produces solutions, results, benefits, profits..." or whatever you have learned that floats the boat of your prospects.

Most companies already have formulated (and most likely spent a lot of money doing so) a proper and particular value proposition, so make that yours until, and if, such time that you find it isn't working for you. Revamp your ownership of it and try again. If it still doesn't work, compare notes with other sale people to see if there is a consensus. If there is, make it management's problem, with proof and validation, of course, and work to be part of the solution.

And, common sense says that being part of the solution rather than part of the problem ensures career longevity.

My Italian grandfather had a saying: "If the wine is bad, throw it out. Never drink bad wine."

CHAPTER 17

The Value Of Value Add

Something I learned while working in the theatre is that a good actor comes to each rehearsal to show that he or she knows the lines and the movements. A finer actor not only shows that he or she has command of the script and blocking, but also brings something fresh and new to demonstrate.

It is one thing to do just what is expected and yet, quite another to do more than expected.

One does not get rewarded or promoted merely by meeting the expectations of the job; one does not even get noticed for doing only that. To be successful in sales or just about anything, the "that's not my job" or "that isn't in my job description" attitudes just don't fly.

Bringing added value to the table is distinctive and re-sets the bar for those just doing the job. Those that recognize the value of the "value add" approach will always have a much higher success rate than those who do not.

And in sales, if one cannot recognize that value or just does merely what was expected most likely has the wrong job or, shouldn't be in sales at all.

Well, then, what is value add? Doing more than expected to provide additional service and benefits to the subject company or customer.

A good mechanic will rotate tires if he notices it is or will soon be needed, even though the only task was to change the oil.

A good accountant will provide a plan for next year's tax preparation when only this year's preparation is required.

A good chef will send out something additional with your meal as he may have come to know your tastes.

The baker will put a thirteenth donut in the bag.

The charter captain will tack on another hour of fishing without charge as he sees how much you are enjoying the experience.

A good sales person will look for an opportunity to provide added value, pursue it, and complete it without expecting anything in return.

A customer worth keeping and loving on will respond most positively to added value actions.

During my career in management for the independent distribution division, I always provided added value, partly because it was my nature to do more than was expected, to never say "that's not my job", and to do a better job than the competition as well as do all I could to increase production and customer satisfaction for both my distributors and their customers.

All of us in my group, as a little band of outlaws, did such things, explaining why we were so successful. We would all deliver most professionally executed product training seminars and sessions; we would deliver excellent and relevant sales training programs; we did field work with new hires to help develop them; we would work closely with distributor customers on solving their problems, and, in general we made ourselves invaluable to the distributors.

In my case, I created "Step O" to help the distributor validate quotas and sales expectations. I created a monthly newsletter of my own that was sort of a combination of Harpers Index and the Readers' Digest regarding latest trends, product data, and the current state of the industry. I also created a monthly real time progress report that showed performance in terms of bookings, deliveries, forecasts, payables, delta to annual quotas, and rebates based on current and estimated performance.

But there was more: I would do what one distributor manager called "homework" assignments. If they were having a problem with a particular sales manager's or sales office's performance, I would be asked to help in what was perceived as a passive manner, but was, in fact, a direct and calculated effort to improve the situation or fix the problem that the management and I had agreed upon previously.

I would also speak up when I knew my product wasn't the right solution for a customer's proposal. Since I did that, which saved my distributors' profits, I was given more opportunities than my competition. My goal was to impact the distributors' bottom line and that was most appealing to them.

So, what do you do?

Here is an interesting example of the value of value add. I knew a young man just starting out in the restaurant business. He had been a short order cook at his family's beanery, and when that was sold he took a job selling for a purveyor, a company that sells supplies and food to restaurants. We had celebrated his new job with several oat sodas at the gin mill where we would meet friends for Friday cocktails.

He was excited and couldn't stop talking about it.

A few weeks later we were again joined over our libations and one of our number asked our young friend why he was missing Friday past.

He told us that he was making his last call of the week at a new restaurant when he learned that the assistant cook hadn't shown up and couldn't be found. He took off his coat and tie, put on an apron, and went to work. He worked the entire dinner crowd that night and that of the following day. Didn't ask for any pay, just saw that his customer needed help and, he helped.

His customer shifted all of his business to my young friend, always spoke highly of him, and gave him referrals regularly. And, that community in the town being tight, he harvested more and more business.

Do what needs doing and then look for more valuable things to do without expecting anything in return. It is another way of loving on your customer and is most altruistic.

CHAPTER 18

Trust: A Noun and A Verb

"In a time of universal deceit—telling the truth
can be a revolutionary act." George Orwell

Another pronouncement that should come as no surprise is that "trust",
as formerly understood, no longer exists. We don't believe anything,
anymore. When was the last time trust existed with anybody, anything,
anywhere not known intimately, up to and including good old western-
civilization-moderne-societal-man-on-top-woman-on-bottom-get-it-
over-with-quick sex...and even then trust is still an issue ("Did you
really have one? Honest?).

A crude example, but it brings the point to a superlative. Trust is a thing,
a concept, and organism that must be present before any relationship
can take the first step. Trust is also an action, an activity, a present and
affirmative sense that solidifies "trust" as a thing.

And in sales, trust is necessary and absolute.

From the beginning of time, from when the hairy Cro-Magnon boys
attempted to sell a haunch of mastodon to the Neanderthals in the next
cave, the prospective buyers were not ready to start a cooking fire until
they could trust the sellers that the meat was fresh, tender, and really
mastodon.

Today, this continues, perhaps stronger than ever, as an era of declining trust in governments and institutions infects most nations. "Vulnerability" is the optimum word when describing trust, as defined by four sociologists (Rousseau, Sitkin, Burt, and Camerer...1998): "Trust is the willingness to accept vulnerability based upon positive expectations about another's behavior". Another way to state "trust" is that it exists when one person is open to rely on the actions of another with the situation directed at what is to come. The first person voluntarily abandons control of the actions of the other while being uncertain of the outcome; expectations are evaluated. Risk is part of the condition. From Lenin we get "Trust is good, control is better."

Establishing trust enables control.

In between seller and buyer, this comes down to establishment of a belief that honesty, fairness, and benevolence exist. As recorded by a recent study, the buyer values confidence and competence above price.

Is this a lot of mumbo-jumbo, shilly-shally talk or is there a basis of truth here? Sociologist Stephen M. R. Covey established "5 waves of trust", that most may find within themselves once they are made aware of them:

1. Credibility. "Do you trust yourself and are you someone that others can trust?"
2. Relationship. This is in regards to your consistent behavior in all your relationships with others; like it or not, others judge us on behavior, not intentions.
3. Organizational. Do your company's structures, policies, and systems align with the trust you endeavor to achieve?
4. Market. Simple, what is your organization's overall reputation? For example, does it stack up against Google "Reviews" both by customers and employees? This can be either a gift or a disaster.
5. Societal. Do your prospects, decision makers, influencers, and ground level users see your organization as having a past record of accomplishment and contribution to the things they care about?

Another pair of sociologists, Martha Lawrence and Ken Blanchard not only compliment Covey's "waves" but further provide elements that are described as "basics and fundamentals" throughout this book.

1. Do you know your stuff and get results?
2. Do you keep your mouth shut, keep confidences, act with knowledge and integrity, and do not hide your knowledge?
3. Do you listen well, demonstrate care and empathy, and solicit input to the decision making process?
4. Do you do what you say you will do? This also means being punctual, consistent, and responsive.

If you find the above resonant, if you can say that you can do that or that you do that regularly, that an understanding and confirmation of trust is within you, it is organic. You have heard of people being "natural" as in flyer, sailor, ball player? To them it is organic, rarely requiring understanding or questioning and manifested without additional thought.

And one last consideration before we continue on with basics and fundamentals: not everyone trusts technology and these people value the face to face communication and interaction with a sales person above all else in the process. By questioning and listening, you will be able to separate the believers from the non-believers.

Trust is a comforting feeling and must exist if reasonable and mutually satisfying arrangements and solutions may be achieved by two parties.

CHAPTER 19

Ethics

"I believe fundamental honesty is the keystone of business." Harvey S. Firestone

"Ethics or simple honesty is the building blocks {sic} upon which our whole society is based, and business is a part of our society, and it's integral to the practice of being able to conduct business, that you have a set of honest standards." Kerry Stokes

"The secret of life is honesty and fair dealing. If you can fake that, you've got it made." Groucho Marx

Starting out in the interconnect business many years ago, I had a senior sales rep preach to my fellow rookies and me: "When all else fails, tell the truth."

Gulp! What had I let myself in for?

Several years later, I heard a manager farther up the food chain exclaim: "The truth is a moving target."

There was another senior sales person who was fond of saying "Never let the truth stand in the way of a good presentation."

Whenever I heard such things from supposedly "successful" and "experienced" sales people I continued to understand why some people are in business in spite of themselves; and, I would walk away shaking my head.

But it takes all kinds to make the world go around, doesn't it?

Want to be successful in the long run? Be honest; be truthful; endeavor to always be ethical. If it is easy, then everyone would be doing it, but that most people don't trust sales people at first blush proves it isn't easy or practiced universally.

"Will it do that, Mr. Buyer? Is that important to you? Yes? Yes, absolutely, it does that. Trust me."

You can drum up hundreds of bromides about truth and honesty and as many about being untruthful and dishonest. What separates the good from the bad and ugly is honesty and truth, as those are constants of people who remain standing after the smoke clears and dust settles.

Why harp on this?

Even if you have a modicum of experience in the world you will agree that unbridled, fundamental human foibles of power, greed, and malice, unfortunately dominate the human condition.

I present career politicians as proof, along with the yellow press, scammers, Ponzi schemers, Enron's, Madoff's, and criminals of all shapes and sizes.

And you will, no doubt, run into any number of prospects, influencers, and buyers who will be short on the truth for a multitude of reasons. Your task is to ferret out such before you have wasted your precious time and energy on erroneously qualified opportunities.

John (Doc) Fabiano

A common prospect/ buyer scam perpetrated upon unsuspecting sales people is to take the information and work the sales person provided and hand it over to the competition. Always ensure the prospect/buyer understands that your work and your proposal are proprietary and are not to be shared.

If the truth of the matter, the issue, the solution, do not make the deal and set you free, then learn from the experience and walk away. There are plenty of opportunities out there for good sales people who are truthful, honest, and maintain a high ethics bar.

Listen to Jimmy Buffett: "Breathe in, breathe out, move on." Good advice.

Do not misrepresent or withhold the truth from a prospective customer. Professionals such as doctors, lawyers, policemen, and more are subject to oversight and discipline from an organized group of their peers to maintain high standards and integrity of the profession. As sales people are professionals as much as others, there should be a similar group.

But there isn't.

So, it is up to you to make sure you are always on the up and up, deliberately and veraciously truthful and honest. It pays off, always, even though one should not be expecting rewards for simply doing the right thing.

Shortly after a Fortune 100 company bought out the original company I worked for, their people brought me and a regional distributor of mine into an opportunity to provide a complete voice and data communications system for a college in the southeast. It was a very large opportunity, but after the specifications of the request for proposal were vetted out, it became clear to the engineers and me that our product was not the most elegant or financially attractive solution.

The product could do what was spec'd, but not without complicated and expensive work-arounds. I did not have enough "discretion" to offer my distributor as a discount to help his profitability.

I met with the distributor EVP and explained the situation and told him that I could not, in good faith, recommend my product as the solution, as the retail price would have to be so low, whatever little profit could be squeezed out would not make the effort worth it and, it would be an expensive problem down the road to resolve.

My EVP could have continued with my competition's product, which his company also marketed, but he made even less profit on that normally, so he made a hard decision to walk away from the deal all together.

Later that year, a huge hospital came up for bid, to include the existing operation as well as a multi-million dollar expansion. My competition threw their biggest "guns" at my EVP and his people to propose their product over mine.

He told them to forget it, it was going to be my product because it fit and I had been straight up about the college deal.

In the end, the hospital turned out to be a much larger financial deal and my distributor made a good profit.

As it is extremely important to be ethical with prospects and customers, so it is extremely important to be ethical in your dealings with your fellow sales people. Never steal or kidnap another sales rep's opportunities, prospects, and/or customers.

It is a prudent idea to keep a journal of your daily efforts, especially to include logging your first contacts and efforts with a new prospect. If your company or sales manager doesn't already have a process or program to record the same, then make sure at least the sales manager knows who you are working with and when you started. This way, you have documented "ownership" of your opportunity and protected it from sales vultures and thieves. Forecasts may accomplish the same thing, but are no guarantee.

Taking another's opportunity while aware that it is theirs and not yours is akin to adultery. It is a sin and manifests unacceptable traits and ethics. Trust and honesty start at home. Some companies will discipline such actions while others will terminate the offender.

Took a call from a customer or prospect that somehow reveals they have been talking to another sales person? Forward it to that sales person. Check to make sure you are not walking into another's sales territory or engaged prospect.

In a struggling economy it is criminal to mess with another person's opportunities.

If you find someone trying to usurp your opportunities, act immediately and bring that activity and your proof of ownership to your management as soon as possible. If the management does nothing, then perhaps you need to consider another job.

"Only a fool fights in a burning house."

CHAPTER 20

Effective Writing

Remember that you can never mean what you say until you can say what you mean. This also includes the written word. A written communication is part of the overall impression your prospect will make of you.

Gertrude Stein once told Ernest Hemmingway that the most difficult thing to do is to write a simple sentence. Granted, old Gertrude had a very elevated opinion of herself and was probably not a great joy to be around, but she came close to the point.

Writing is not as simple as one may think. It requires command of the language, knowledge of spelling and punctuation, organization, commitment to the message, among other disciplines as well as a great deal of proofreading and an understanding of editing.

Compared to many of the world's languages, English does come off pretty screwed up, but in this country it is all we have, so, get over it and learn it. It really isn't that difficult if you can ignore logic.

Do not expect your first draft to be the final copy; that is rather conceited. Good writers go through many re-writes until they get it right. (George Segal once said of writers: "Why are they called writers? Because they are always right.")

We all remember (hopefully) what we first learned in English class: who, what, why, where, when, and how. It is a simple organizational outline to keep in mind. Who am I writing to? What am I trying to say? Why am I trying to say it? Where is it important? When is it most important? How am I going to convey my message? And there are paragraphs of other ways to do the same thing.

But there is another "constant" that you should keep in mind: the basic message, speech, and presentation order. Tell them what you are going to tell them. Tell them. Tell them you told them. It is a simple arc and it presents the message three times, which most brain-shrinkers will tell you is the minimum the human needs to hear or read something to absorb it.

So, before you start pounding the keys consider the previous two paragraphs twice more.

The LA Business Journal has reported that billions of dollars are lost due to insufficient writing skills among business people. Billions. Why? Poor writing creates an immediate poor first impression and, in business, you don't get second impressions.

Google will respond with over 37 million hits as you search "business writing". There must be something to it then. But it doesn't have to be overwhelming if you give yourself credit for having a brain, the ability to create thoughts, and practice a few simple steps.

That you should know spelling and grammar is absolute. Don't trust any spellcheck app. Get yourself a good dictionary or Google anything you are unsure of. Owning a thesaurus (not a dinosaur, but a language aid close to extinction) is an excellent idea.

Not only keep what you are writing simple, but keep it concise and to the point. Leave verbosity to James Joyce and the transcendentalist writers of the 17 and 1800's. Start by putting everything in you think is relative to your message, then spend serious time taking out everything that does not directly go the message. Less is more; give your reader credit for having a brain and an imagination. Overdoing it is condescending and nobody likes being looked down upon.

Know who you are writing to. Know your audience. What do you know that elicits a response from that particular person positively? What do you know that annoys them? Stay away from that. What are they interested in relative to your communication? What is it that person expects to read? How strong is that person's command of the language?

As you prepare, use the "who-what-why-where-when-how" string to help you establish a tighter message and what should go where. Consider this string first to "who". What do you know about this person? What is he/she like? What are obvious traits and habits? Is this person verbose or shy? Is this person hard or soft; stiff or loose; condescending or agreeable?

When you know something about your reader, you will first understand how and what not to write. Considering that, then work at how to write to appeal to that person. Formal; colloquial; humorous; light; strictly factual; sparsely; what you think makes sense to best get your point across to that person.

Don't use jargon, abbreviations, buzzwords, clichés or condensing initials (BMI. ROI, STD, and the like). Avoid glossy adjectives and adverbs; write directly, as you would speak. Considering your writing as a conversation is generally a better way to communicate; it will put your reader at ease. Don't end sentences with prepositions; avoid beginning sentences with "I" as much as possible. Try not to use the same word more than once in a sentence and paragraph.

To give your sentences a sense of "now" (immediacy), use action verbs and write in the present tense. Try to avoid passivity in words, clauses, and sentences as much as possible. Maintain not only the present tense throughout, but also maintain the pronouns as well: don't start with "one does this" and then write "you should do this" or go from the singular pronoun he, she, it, me, you, to the plural: them, they, their.

"Who" is a person; "that" or "this" is a thing. "Whom" is a possessive of who, a person; "its" is possessive of a thing or things. "it's" is the contraction of "it is". Avoid contractions as much as possible.

Paragraph one, the opening paragraph, is really an agenda for the rest of the communication, starting with a condensation of the most important point and then, on in order of declining importance.

Now, move from general to specific.

The following paragraph or paragraphs will then elaborate on each point, in order, but in a concise and simple format. Here validate with the "why", the benefit, the need. Start with a topic sentence, an active verb sentence about the main point and then continue to elaborate.

The closing paragraph is a condensed summary of what has already been written, emphasizing the value of the subject matter, as well as inviting questions.

Now, proof read, edit, repeat, several times. A good way to proof read is to read from start to finish and then from finish to start. Reading something backwards is an excellent way to discover mistakes in spelling and grammar, as well as syntax. Ask a peer or your sales manager to proofread it. It is also an idea common amongst writers to let the piece "sit" or "simmer" for a day or two. You would be surprised what a difference that can make.

Business writing as a general rule is formal and factual as well as spelling and grammatically perfect. Knowing your reader will allow you to pursue a style that is more you and prone to attracting and keeping the interest of that person. Certainly, your writing style may be looser with your daily contact than that you use to communicate with the president of the company.

Avoid stilted writing that you are uncomfortable with. If you don't like it, how can you expect someone else, to whom you want to get the message, to like it as well.

Something else to consider: you will never sell to someone you don't like or understand and, vis a vie, a prospect won't buy from someone he/she doesn't like or understand. First and ongoing impressions are critical to success.

Keep it simple and spare. Practice writing the message, the point, concisely, with the audience in mind and complete command of your subject.

Read, don't stop reading. Read what others have written. Steal (but do not plagiarize) what you like and believe works and make it yours. And always keep copies of what you have written and sent out.

A simple and purposeful exercise is to write about a subject, considering an "arc" and using the above methods to 500 words. Then, after an hour or more, come back and edit it down to 250 words. Then later come back to edit to 100 words.

The results you get will be quite interesting.

CHAPTER 21

Polished Communications

Any good relationship thrives on good communications. Try going a week without speaking to your spouse and see what happens.

Sales is no different.

All meetings should be confirmed in writing with a proposed or expected agenda. Following the meeting another document should detail the discussion, confirm any agreements, and propose a date for the next meeting.

It is simply good manners and manifests a high degree of professionalism without much effort.

The question is, swimming in all of the communications technology available from email to several social media venues, which is the appropriate venue to choose for formal contact with the prospect/customer?

Granted, my hair and moustache have been silver for many years, but experience has shown me that there is a time and place for everything (and don't forget my earlier words about questioning…everything, as well as making it yours). I found that a professional looking, hand addressed envelope containing a well written communication on good quality stationery stands out from anything else and is more likely to be taken seriously.

But, in today's world, that is for you to decide. Taking the time to get to know your prospect will help with your choices.

There should be a sequential series of communications (direct mail or electronic) throughout the entire sales process. It can also be used to provide increased confidence and trust. Certainly, a communication confirming the meeting set as a result of the first phone call is required. That is just SOP (Standard Operating Procedure).

Following that meeting, it is prudent to compose a confirming memo regarding what was discussed, what was agreed upon, if anything, tasks that may be required prior to the next meeting, and the place, time, and date of that next meeting.

But here is a place to simply start locking things in place: list what you have discerned as the prospect's reasons to buy. These are solvable needs as described by your prospect. Follow this list with a simple statement that you recognize these as "reasons to buy" or "reasons to do business together" when your company provides those solutions and/ or meets those needs.

You will find out a lot from this letter. If there are any objections to this early point in the process, they will appear. If the prospect returns with cancelling the next meeting, what does that tell you? Get right back with a letter or a phone call that simply asks "why?" And keep asking why until you get your answer or have concluded that this is not a qualified prospect.

Assuming the memo is received with a go ahead to the next step, the next meeting, then here introduce the "track" (see Appendix 3) if you have not already and prepare a draft of one for discussion at the next meeting.

In the meantime, it is not a bad idea to have your sales management send a communication to the prospect indicating that he/she is aware of this opportunity, acknowledges he/she will be involved, looks forward to their meeting, that you are a fine person and well qualified, and that he/she is always at his/her service.

Polish.

While you continue to follow up each meeting with a confirming memo, consider introducing the rest of your "team" that will be involved in the process of the survey (discovery), analysis, design, installation, training, and on-going maintenance. Do this with a letter from each to that person's appropriate counterpart within the prospect's company as well as a copy to your point of contact.

Establishing dialog between these people is most valuable to establishing confidence, trust, validation, and other good feelings about the opportunity and for your prospect to look like a hero for getting solutions to problems and needs.

All of this is the tail end of what some call "nurturing".

Build a solid relationship with your prospect from the beginning; becoming BFFs (Best Friends Forever) is not the goal here, but a positive business relationship is built upon mutual respect. It is unfortunate however, that this is not a two- sided effort and it is incumbent upon the sales person to start this relationship.

Relative to "relationships" and good communications there are some prospects that will take advantage of the relationship for "entertainment" or "perks" a sales person may provide and come to expect the dinners, the golf rounds, the fishing trips, and the like. The sales person needs to be wary and come to a high degree of confidence in the opportunity before expending any of his T & E (Travel & Expense) budget. However, there are other prospects and customers where such "perks" are a good demonstration of gratitude and grateful people are always well liked.

You decide. Question. A good question to keep asking yourself is the expense, the demonstration of sincerity, worth the result? How do such actions work as a quid pro quo?

My Southeast distributor had a large banking operation as a customer and since the bank was expanding by leaps and bounds, all of my competition and that of my distributor where all over the bank's management. What they didn't know was the primary influencer, who was just a tick shy of signing checks (and as the IT head, got whatever he wanted) and I had become a friends as we shared many common interests. Whenever I was in town, we would get together for a nice dinner, which was divided between discussing business and fun.

What was nice was that I knew he trusted me and I trusted him.

To ensure what would be a great deal of business in the coming year, I made him an offer: purchase 'x' amount of my product from my distributor and when that number was reached, I would take him and my distributor's sales rep to a fine golf resort north of our corporate headquarters in the Silicon Valley.

My friend surpassed the target and revealed what had been future "secret" expansion plans. The outing was a success and I even set up a meeting with some higher ups in my company so they could compliment my friend and thank him for his loyalty.

The cost of the outing compared to the secured opportunity and those to come was what we called then "mice nuts"....tiny things.

But, again, it is your decision.

CHAPTER 22

To Stay or to Go

As sales is, at its most basic, a numbers exercise, prudent use of time is paramount. Sales people are professionals of the same phylum and species as lawyers, accountants, doctors, carpenters, plumbers, HVAC repair people, and any other profession that requires skill and education and charges by the hour.

But sales people are not paid by the hour, you say. Or are they? Here is a simple exercise: via your journal, keep track of your time from prospect to close of any recent accomplishment. Suppose it took you a sum total of 60 hours to close a deal that earned you $1200 in commission; you were "earning" $20 an hour. But suppose, after 60 hours, you didn't get the contract? What did that produce: $0.00 an hour or a negative number.

A good sales person makes the best use of his/her time, always, and never spends time on questionable prospects. High performers will not spend any more time after the first meeting with a prospect they highly suspect, or simply know from experience, is not qualified, or, in some instances, is not going to be worth the time, effort, and profit.

A real estate agent will refer to such prospects as "Looky Lou's"; a seasoned car sales person will "broom" such unqualified lookers off of the lot as politely and as quickly as possible. And there are hundreds of other expressions about evading the unqualified, the simply curious, and the indecisive.

Indecisive? Yes, you will come across supposed opportunities where the prospect is simply curious and, no matter what, is probably not going make a decision in your lifetime.

These folks are tremendous time-wasters and can suck up a beginner sales person's time faster than a plutonium powered vacuum cleaner.

As a professional, working daily to be better than the day before, it is important to master the fundamentals, of which qualifying is a high priority. You have a brain, use it. Talk to the sales manager, the seasoned, high performers; read and research techniques if you are either in the dark or twilight.

But don't sit there figuring it out yourself if you haven't done it before.

Arthur Conan Doyle made Sherlock Holmes the detective of all detectives by giving him unparalleled powers of observation. Nothing escaped Holmes' attention and that was his super power; he made connections from what he had and had not seen and heard.

So, keep your eyes and ears open, especially on that first call. You are looking for signs of financial stability, as well as financial ability to pay, need, ability to make decisions, seriousness, and hints at possible collaboration, among other glaring things.

A new, young sales person asked me to accompany her on a first call to a company she had gotten on a referral. It didn't sound like a big opportunity, but it is always a smart plan to make time to get the rookies off to a good start.

The owner didn't introduce himself or us to the four other people unfolding chairs and sitting in a circle in a cramped room. He didn't shake hands, and just announced that he owed the person who referred him a favor so we had better get "off of our asses and get on with whatever it was we thought we could sell him." He then went into a tirade about disliking sales people as all were liars and not to be trusted, especially guys wearing suits and Rolex watches, which was a direct shot at me. He then announced that he would not be sold anything just because the rookie was a "hot blonde with nice tits".

I made polite apologies for taking up his valuable time, and, after telling him I was unaccustomed to having my integrity questioned, I grabbed my rookie and calmly walked out of the nearest exit.

I doubted that man could ever be sold, but if he could be, he would require an extremely high cost of maintenance. Let the competition go broke trying to please him.

An extreme example, perhaps, but the point is made; don't try to swim upstream, fight in a burning house, or tug on Superman's cape. The better part of valor and making better use of time was to breathe in, breathe out, and move on to more fertile ground and reasonably polite prospects.

Many sales people, far more than you may realize, throw away time by attending to prospects that are long shots, if closable at all.

Why?

Because it looks and feels like work and such provides a false sense of accomplishment. However, it indicates ineffective and poor habits to include lack of experience, trying to make something that didn't work, work, and (and sorry to say this) fear of failure. Continuing down such a path is denial and is simply throwing what could have been time better used down after wasted time.

Einstein said that repeating the same thing over and over, expecting a different result, is a definition of insanity.

There is another concern, however and that is the person that is so competitive, he/she won't give up even though the horse is dead. Clint Eastwood said in one of his movies: "A man has got to know his limitations".

This comes with experience, but comes quicker if you keep track of activities via a daily journal and are not hesitant about asking the more experienced for advice and help. Let's complete the metaphor: don't beat a dead horse.

Another concern is the inexperienced sales manager who insists his reps continue working accounts that the reps know are a waste of time. Wanting his/her people to never "give up" may be a noble desire but it is not always realistic. How do you deal with that?

Bring your sales manager to a meeting with the prospect you are trying to dump from your forecast and let the truth come out then. If the sales manager doesn't recognize the situation, or (as anything is possible) can't make the sale, then you have a choice to make: stop working the deal regardless or, stop working for the sales manager.

To work smart, you have to know how to work smart, and learning to qualify quickly will allow you to make better use of your time and work opportunities that you can secure.

But never walk away from any "unqualified" opportunity with anything less than good relations and always open for future communication. Sometimes the strangest things can happen.

One of my distributors had a very good customer who had been with the distributor from the beginning of his business. This customer started selling sports equipment out of his garage and got his telephone service from my distributor. As he grew, so did his telephony needs, which the distributor excellently provided. A classic, seminal, good provider/ customer business relationship existed.

There came a time when the "big" move up was to be made, calling for a much larger system with expandable call center capabilities. We responded with the best we had, but never assumed that the business was ours, a fait accompli.

Professional.

The competition came in and undercut us by over 30%. We didn't think their solution would work for that price and after giving all of my discount discretion to the distributor and the distributor lowering his price, we were still considerably apart.

We went in for one last meeting to let the customer know we were at the end of our pricing capabilities, and, after all the years of growing and being together, we were sorry to lose him. We wished him the very best of luck, thanked him for all of his business and left.

Shortly after we returned, glum, to the distributor's offices, while commiserating over coffee, we got a call from the customer.

"To hell with those other guys. We have been together far too long to be apart so get back over here with the contract. Let's do it."

Sometimes you never know; keep your options open; be fair, honest, and empathetic.

CHAPTER 23

The Journal

One of the major problems with history is the only thing we have learned from history is that we haven't learned much, if anything, from history.

Statistics show that 65% of sales people finish calls without asking for the order, as well as make sales call on the wrong person. 85% of sales people do not generate enough referrals, much less actually ask for them, which is sad, as it is estimated that over 90% of buyers will offer them. 80% of sales opportunities are lost because of failure to establish trust and credibility. Almost half of all sales people give up after the first call, yet many others will continue working a clearly unqualified prospect.

A couple of other things have happened in the last decade or so: buyers are moving away from industry publications and, a brand is no longer what the company tells the customers it is, but rather it is what customers tell each other it is.

Inbound marketing and network marketing have become the most efficient methods of securing qualified prospects and cold calling from cold lists or knocking on doors continues to be proven a poor use of time.

Referrals remain the best source of prospects, but since most don't ask for them, the explanation that only 11% or so that do are the high performers isn't that difficult to understand.

This was stated earlier, but it is worth stating it again: doing the same thing over and over again and expecting a different result is the definition of insanity, according to Albert Einstein.

Kind of hard to argue with old Albert.

History has proven, over and over, that in any given situation, the simplest solution is the best. So, it makes sense that keeping things simple and keeping to the fundamentals are not only the paths of least resistance, but are also the most effective.

How do you get better?

Use your brain and learn from your mistakes. If you haven't closed anything in a while, but the rest of your peers have, that is a pretty good indication that something isn't working for you.

Think.

Where and when did things change for the worst? What did you do that brought an end to your chances of making the most of an opportunity? Why is it taking you a long time to secure a prospect?

You must be coldly and brutally honest with yourself. If you recognize that something you are doing or not doing isn't working and you resolve to fix it, you have taken the first and absolutely correct step. Acknowledging the problem opens the door to repair.

You have to look backwards; you have to compile experiences; you have to be able to trace your steps.

And this is where the journal comes in.

Granted, some people have a problem journaling for any number of erroneous rationalizations but it is the simplest way of getting things fixed. If you can't measure it, you can't manage it and if you can't manage it, you can't fix it.

So, get yourself a journal you can carry with you: a spiral bound notebook or a more purpose built diary, anything with pages that can be kept in order and dated.

Get into the habit of writing down your daily activities as your last task of the day, if you haven't been writing things down all through the day. You don't need to write a short story or a novel, but you do need to write down the facts: When, where, what, why, how, with who and, what happened.

You may wish to keep a separate section for each opportunity you work to keep things organized. Date your activities, from start to finish. Describe, factually, what you did, and in many cases, what was said by you and the prospect. Go back and review frequently.

Set up a simple spread sheet to keep numerical track: dates, duration in days from start to finish, steps accomplished, steps missed or dismissed, who was who on the prospect's food chain. When the opportunity is finished, whether with a contract or a loss, calculate the time taken and compare to other deals lost or won. Out of 10 opportunities, how many did you close? That is your closing ratio.

Not getting enough business? Maybe you are taking too long to either walk away or get to closure. Look at your time line to understand. Look at your prospecting results; how can you secure more appointments, how can you improve your closing ratio? Where is your time going?

If you are spending more than 50 hours a week and not getting to quota, up your time about 10% for a month.

After a month or two, if things are not getting better, you have a good indication that this job isn't for you. Walk away and find something suitable to your aptitude and talents.

Never be afraid to walk away.

Performance is the key to longevity and if that isn't there, time will be short.

Don't ever be afraid to ask for help, for evaluations of your work. A good manager is eager to help his/her people get better and admitting you need help or admitting there must be things you don't know are good steps towards improvement.

If your sales manager is not working with you, not going on calls with you, or is just flat out not interested to make time for you, leave.

Only a fool fights in a burning house.

Having the journal will allow you to track, diagram, or chart your activities and results in any number of ways that may make sense to you and someone else.

Another advantage of keeping a journal is it establishes ownership so no one else can try to take your opportunity. The journal indicates when you started, what you have done, so, if you are working at it, no one can say you are ignoring the opportunity.

Remember an ancient law of business: he/she who has the best notes, wins.

Remember that a true professional is never satisfied with his/her current performance and is always striving to be better. In the sales world, you are only as good as what you did last month, last week, or yesterday. If you are in an industry where sales require more than a day or two and more than one call, consider leaving if you are measured constantly by what you did in the morning; that just isn't realistic.

Confidence is a key attribute of a successful sales person. A healthy ego is a key attribute. Strength of character and will are also necessary characteristics. Understand what it is you do well, what it is you love doing, and find a way to get paid for doing it.

CHAPTER 24

The Loyal Opposition

Now that you are ready to go forth into the world, ready to succeed, you must remember you are not the only fish in the sea. And before you venture out you must know who, what, and where the other fish are.

See yourself as an apex predator: top of the food chain.

You may find the competition hawking like products and services few or many, depending on the products, services, and needs. Most of the time it is many, or, it certainly seems that way.

Who are these guys and where did they come from?

Sometimes from right in front of you, sometimes from under rocks, sometimes flown in from distant circles, and sometimes, right next door. Regardless, it is incumbent you to know more about them than they know about you, otherwise you will end up with the dirty end of the stick and that end of the stick smells.

Yes, you can lose your deal to the loyal opposition in many, many different ways if you haven't done your homework and haven't kept your eyes and ears open, as well as qualify, qualify, qualify, and repeat.

Chances are your competition is offering the same things you are but with a different spin. In commodity sales this is a given: in insurance sales there is not a lot of difference, as it is a regulated industry and one needs a license to sell. With water softeners there is the device and the salt to make the water, well, softer. Not a lot of room for difference here. Vacuums pretty much all do the same thing (they all suck) but vary a lot in price. The same is with cars: they all can get you to where you want to go and the hot points are very similar.

Within the communications industry it started with who had the most features. Then it became whose system had the most memory. Then came computer clock speed followed shortly by bandwidth and "mtbf" (mean time between failures). Suddenly two pair cable replaced 24 pair cable to each telephone and those became "devices" as tone pads could now be used as keyboards since the new systems now carried data on top of voice which led to copper cable being replaced by glass fiber which is being replaced by "wifi" and the internet. It used to be there was between three to six months before products were replaced by new and better machines; now it may be argued it is less than 24 hours. If my team and I did not keep up with the latest changes and developments almost daily, we would have been left way behind.

Not much different throughout the information industry. But now service provided by software has become the new race track with the major players doing all they can to lead by a length.

I wonder how long it will be until the Vegas odds makers start taking bets on who and what will be the next leader.

Yes, it is a tangled jungle of competitors out there and you must find your path through it.

But the first thing you need to learn is this: never, ever, bad-mouth the loyal opposition. You are not a politician running a campaign for some office. Leave the bad-mouthing to the competition, republicans, and democrats. You only mention them when asked what the difference is between you and them. Then reference what makes you and your product more valuable to the prospect. By talking "smack" you only hurt yourself, you lose credibility as a professional, as someone who has unquestionable command of his product and the process, and all that takes is one misspoken word. Don't do it.

Commodities boil down to price and service; cost of ownership may also be a constant. For all competition, for all products and services, you need to know the competition's products and services at least as good as they do, but preferably better. And not just the nuts and bolts of it, but performance in the field, the market place.

This is where your skills at research come in. Scour the internet. Write an email to their marketing or sales departments and, as a professional for a certain company, you would like to know how it works, what the differences are with other like products, what it costs, and where the value lies.

Most companies, including yours, tout benefits, value, service, and more on their websites. Pricing is another stone to over-turn and you will need to use your creative powers to secure this information.

Regardless of the product or service, make yourself a comparison chart of who offers what and what is the same and what is different. You may choose to use this as a sales tool, but only if you are absolutely positive and confident that it is perfect. Remember: research—just another way of finding answers to as yet unasked questions.

Certainly, there is a difference between price and value. Price is what it costs once. Value is what it brings to the prospect in terms of increased business, lower overhead, efficiency, cost of ownership, aftermarket development and upgrades, service, and any other "hot buttons" you have unearthed.

Working with major private telephone companies across the nation I learned that by keeping overhead low and securing large market shares, they had more money in the bank than any of the competition.

I frequently found myself in an awkward position where my company's direct sales forces' territory overlapped that of my distributors. There were times when the direct group would play the "factory direct" card with the prospect as justification for a higher price and then come down, to sometimes under my telephone company's price.

Earning the business over the direct group was simple: we made cost of ownership the crucial factor. That is to say, we demonstrated to the prospect that while the offerings were the same, ours was considerably cheaper in the long run as the telephone company's post warranty service contracts were generally half of the direct group's.

The telephone company had the infrastructure to allow that to happen and still make a profit. We used to say that if the telephone company bought a snorkel truck today, it had been paid for a month ago.

It is then worthwhile to consider preparing and presenting a cost analysis once you have determined how the company handles expenditures for the purchase of what you are offering. How is it to be financed? Cash sale or lease? How is the purchase structured on the balance sheet? Operating expense? How will this affect the tax liabilities? Where will the purchase demonstrate savings? Overhead? Personnel? Efficiency? Increased sales? Greater profitability? Will it allow your prospect to "leap frog" his competition? Life time cost of ownership?

There are many ways to decimalize the value of your product or service. It is up to you to ask the right questions and come to understand how to assemble what you have learned and present it in a simple, but fluid format. Excel can be valuable here as it is extremely flexible, allowing you to make changes instantly and produce any number of "what if's". You must have ownership of such things.

Review, review, review. By doing so you deny the chance of mistakes and surprises.

Always do a better, more thorough job than your competition, something that differentiates you from them.

One of my telephone companies was planning another big call center and sent the "rfp" (request for proposal) only to my competition and me, as it could purchase what it needed at cost.

A couple of things happened: although the company marketed both my product and the competition's, I knew my company's needs and likes better. I also know they appreciated hard work and thoroughness. So, I went to work as if it was a normal prospect "rfp" out in the world. I did not take this opportunity as a fait accompli.

I surveyed all involved for needs, current plans, future plans, and goals. I knew this purchase would be on the "short list" of the company's financial plans and I knew what it took to make the list. I learned what they had now and I asked how they wanted the new system designed and work. Along the way I enlisted the help and support of the engineers, the call center management, the end users, and the financial people. We knew each other anyway, and to work smart, one should always look for opportunities to make partners.

All of this went into my proposal, including template examples of how the telephones in their call centers looked now and how they would look with my product in place. I included a financial and work analysis and how my product could reduce holding times, allowing their agents to service more customers.

When I finished, there was not one rock I had not turned over. My proposal was complete and in a three-inch binder.

My competition handed in two pages: a list of hardware and software and the net price, expecting an easy sale. I know, because the EVP showed me.

And who do you suppose walked away with the business?

I wrote earlier that one of the qualities a salesperson must have is to not be afraid of hard work.

Go back to Chapter 2 "The salesperson's index": "A buyer values competence over quality of offering, over the solution recommended, and least of all, price."

The loyal opposition can be tough and aggressive, but there are several techniques you may use to further establish yourself as the person on top.

Never allow yourself to be roped into a one-on-one, face to face competition, with your opposition. This will always generate into a you- know-what contest and come down to a tit-for-tat volley that accomplishes nothing.

Let the competition make mistakes either by managing them into it, or just keeping your eyes and ears open. Capitalize on such, but in a positive manner where you lead the prospect into making that discovery himself.

Remain professional throughout, and agreeable and personable all the time. If you have done your homework, you will understand what the prospect responds to not only positively but also negatively.

Buyers value personalization, so while keeping things professional, allow a "patina" of personalization flow over your process. Do not be ramrod straight about things. Allow the prospect to talk as long as he wants. Never outright disagree with your prospect regardless how ridiculous he may become. Make sure he knows you are listening: letting him see you take notes and take the time to confirm things is an excellent way to do this.

When appropriate, keep things light, and, again, when appropriate, encourage your prospect to talk about him or herself, which is every person's favorite subject.

People are in a higher acceptable state when they have reached conclusions on their own. To that end, lead your prospect into his or her own discovery of what is important, what is valuable, and why your product, solution, or service is better.

Using a sales track will demonstrate that you are highly organized. Always do what you say you will do, on schedule, on time, and with a little bit extra.

Find out how your competition works, what is strong and what is weak and capitalize on what you have learned. Let the customer discover the weaknesses by maneuvering to that subject.

Beware of amateurs as they can be unpredictable. You must have the will and the knowledge to elegantly roll over them while letting them display their inexperience and ignorance.

You have nothing to fear from the competition but your uncertainties and anxieties which you can overcome by doing your homework. Churchill said "We have not come this far by being made of cotton candy." You are not made of such fluff, but much stronger stuff. Your competition is no better than you, puts pants on one leg at a time, and wants the same thing you do: the deal, the contract, the business.

Think of Hunter S. Thompson's famous quote: "When the going gets weird, the weird turn pro." Now, substitute "tough" for "weird" and you are on your way.

EPILOGUE

Regardless of the resonance you have or have not found herein, go forth, with great confidence to succeed, to keep learning, to use your brain, to question, to keep things simple, and to always do the right thing. Revel in your success's and learn from your failures. Embrace what you do well and endeavor to earn a living doing it. Have no fear and believe in yourself.

APPENDIX #1

Sample Worksheet

1	**STEP 0**	**MANAGING TO THE BUSINESS**			
2	**B**	**C**	**D**	**E**	**F**
3	TOTAL MARKET			2000	2000
4	LIFE CYCLE (YEARS)			5	5
5	POTENTIAL AVAILABLE MARKET			400	400
6	AVERAGE CLOSING RATIO			20%	30%
7	ANTICIPATED CLOSED MARKET			100	120
8	AVERAGE DEAL AT RETAIL			$250,000	$250,000
9	AVERAGE SALES CYCLE PER PROPOSAL/ MONTHS)			2	1
10	ANTICIPATED ANNUAL SALES VOLUME			$25,000,000	$30,000,000
11	PROPOSALS/MONTH CARRIED BY @ REP			4	4
12	TOTAL ANNUAL			24	48
13	CLOSED PROPOSALS @ CLOSING RATIO			6	12
14	ANTICIPATED ANNUAL REP PRODUCTION			$1,500,000	$3,000,000
15	ESTIMATED REQUIRED SALES REPS			16.67	10

Step 0 Small Company

AVAILABLE MARKET	120000	DEMOGRAPHICS
TARGET ANNUAL GOAL	$2,000,000	ARBITRARY
AVG CONTRACT $$	$8,000	HISTORIC
CLOSED DEALS RQ'D	250	($2M/$8000)
CLOSING RATIO	25%	HISTORIC
PROPOSALS REQ'D	1000	(25%/250)
PROPOSAL LOAD/REPMO.	5	HISTORIC
ANNUAL PROPOSALS/REP	60	(5*12)
REPS RQ'D	17	(1000/60=16.7)
CLOSED PROPOSALS/REP/YR	15	(60*.25)
ANNUAL REP VOLUME	$120,000	(15*$8000)
PERFORMANCE TO TARGET	$2,040,000	($120000*17)
COLD CALL HRS=1 APPT	6.25	(@8CALLS/HR)
REQ'D HRS. MO.	31.25	(6.25*5)
APPTS TO PROPOSALS RATIO	25%	(ARBITRARY)
APPTS. TO PROPOSALS/MO.	20	(5/25%)
ADJUSTED COLD CALL HRS	125	(6.25*20)
AVAILABLE HRS/MO.	172	(40*4.3 WEEKS)
% TIME COLD CALLING	71%	(125/175)
TTL CLOSED DEALS	255	(15*17)
ANNUAL MARKET IMPACT	0.002	(255/120000)

APPENDIX #3

The Sales Track

The sales track is a most simple method for controlling the process as well as demonstrating high degree of professionalism and locking the prospect into a series of subtle trial closes.

While the track should be kept simple, it should break down all of the major tasks required to reach solutions and satisfaction. It may take a while to nail everything down as well as who does what when and how long each task will take, but usually a well-planned meeting of an hour or two should suffice. That is, of course, well-planned by the sales person.

On the sales side, prior to meeting with the prospect, the sales person needs to communicate with all parties involved as to what needs to be done, who does what, how long will it take, and how much notice is required.

One of the nice values of the sales track is it requires multiple "sanctions" from the prospect to the employees which is a notification from management of specific tasks to be accomplished by both the sales group and prospect personnel. This subtly shortens the path towards the "fait accompli" the track develops. Always get confirmation, agreement, and approval as each task is completed and before the next is begun. It is not a bad idea to have the prospect initial (in each "TASK" box) as the task is completed.

A representative track may look like this for a proposed sale of a lower middle range communications system.

Notice that the "purchase order" is not the last task listed.

XYZ--SALES ABC--CUSTOMER

WHO	TASK/LOCATION		DATE
XYZ/ABC	TASK PLANNING/TIME LINE ABC OFFICES	3 HRS	1/11/
ALL	REVIEW TRACK/ Q&A ABC OFFICES	3 HRS	1/14/
ABC	COMPILE BILLS/INVOICES ABC OFFICES	3 DAYS	1/20/
ALL	REVIEW/VALIDATE BILLS/ INVOICES ABC OFFICES	3 HRS	1/24/
ABC/XYZ	REVIEW DECISION PROCESS ABC OFFICES	2 HRS	1/25/
ABC	SANCTION MEMO TO ABC EMPLOYEES RE: SURVEY ABC OFFICES	1 HR	1/26/
XYZ	SURVEY PLANNING XYZ OFFICES	2 HRS	1/27/
XYZ/ABC	SURVEY ABC OFFICES	1 DAY	1/28/
XYZ	COMPILE/ANALYZE SURVEY XYZ OFFICES	1 DAY	1/30/
XYZ/ABC	REVIEW SURVEY FINDINGS ABC OFFICES	4 HRS	2/2/
XYZ	SOLUTION DESIGNS XYZ OFFICES	1 DAY	2/4/
XYZ	SOLUTIONS TESTED & VALIDATED XYZ	1 DAY	2/6/

XYZ/ABC	REVIEW SOLUTIONS FOR ACCEPTANCE ABC OFFICES	4 HRS	2/8/
ABC/XYZ	DEMONSTRATE SOLUTIONS XYZ CUSTOMER LOCATION	4 HRS	2/10/
XYZ	PROPOSAL BUILD XYZ OFFICES	1 DAY	2/12/
XYZ/ABC	PROPOSAL DELIVERY ABC OFFICES	4 HRS	2/14/
ABC	PURCHASE ORDER ISSUED	1 HR	2/15/
XYZ	INSTALL SCHEDULE REVIEWED DELIVERED TO ABC	2 HRS	
XYZ	INSTALL ABC OFFICES	5 DAYS	2/20/
XYZ/ABC	PRODUCT TRAINING ABC OFFICES	1 DAY	2/22/
ABC	REVIEW/ACCEPTANCE ABC OFFICES	3 HRS	2/26/
XYZ	FOLLOW-UP	4 HRS	2/27/
XYZ/ABC	REFERRALS/ RECOMMENDATIONS	3 HRS	3/1/

ABOUT THE AUTHOR

John Fabiano put himself through college working summers at yacht clubs and marinas in the Hamptons. He graduated college with degrees in the arts and theatre and post graduate degrees in Performing Arts Management and Play Direction and was a Graduate Fellow at Wayne State's prestigious Hilberry Repertory Theatre. Prior to entering the corporate world, he developed audiences for several different performing arts venues.

He has said that the business of show business is simple as it is "an ass in every seat, providing there is a good product on the stage."

In his lifetime he has sold radio advertising, vacuums, violets, Volvos, and other various products and services. He owned a billiard parlor-tavern, held credentials as a financial advisor, taught special education in an autistic unit, and delivered seminars on pre-need funeral arrangements.

He ascended from the position of a sales engineer directly to increasing levels of sales management, eventually reaching the position of National Sales Manager for a global communications company. During that period he consistently qualified for performance above plan recognitions and bonuses.

A former avid sailor and fisherman, John, (who goes by "Doc" to his friends) has traveled extensively, cruised the Bahamas, fished a couple of oceans and seas, swam with and lassoed sharks in Bora Bora, was awed by the Northern Lights in Anchorage, witnessed the green sunset flash from Moorea, watched Mona Kea erupt from a small plane, and lounged, beer in hand, in a hammock watching a Tahitian dance group rehearse on a black sand beach in Papeete among other eclectic experiences.

He got his first writing job at 16, covering the waterfront for his hometown weekly newspaper for the grand sum of $.50 a column inch.

Today an artist and writer, John lives in Jacksonville, Florida with his wife, Beth, herself a top performer in her industry.

"Buy the ticket, take the ride." Hunter S. Thompson

www.ingramcontent.com/pod-product-compliance
Lightning Source LLC
Chambersburg PA
CBHW031055180526
45163CB00002BA/842